INVADERS AND INFIDELS

INVADERS AND INFIDELS

FROM SINDH TO DELHI: THE 500-YEAR JOURNEY OF ISLAMIC INVASIONS

BOOK 1

SANDEEP BALAKRISHNA

Copyright © 2024 Sandeep Balakrishna

Sandeep Balakrishna has asserted his rights under the Indian Copyright Act to be identified as the author of this work.

All rights reserved under the copyright conventions. No part of this publication may be reproduced or transmitted in any form or by any means, electronic or mechanical, including photocopying, recording or any information storage or retrieval system, without the prior permission in writing from the publisher.

This book is solely the responsibility of the author(s) and the publisher has had no role in the creation of the content and does not have responsibility for anything defamatory or libellous or objectionable.

BluOne Ink Pvt. Ltd does not have any control over, or responsibility for, any third-party websites referred to in this book. All internet addresses given in this book were correct at the time of going to press. The author and publisher regret any inconvenience caused if addresses have changed or sites have ceased to exist, but can accept no responsibility for any such changes.

ISBN: 978-81-968471-2-8

First published in India 2024
This edition published 2024

BluOne Ink Pvt. Ltd
A-76, 2nd Floor, Sector 136, Noida
Uttar Pradesh 201301
www.bluone.ink
publisher@bluone.ink

Kali, Occam and BluPrint are all trademarks of BluOne Ink Pvt. Ltd.

To
Ammu for the rock-solid support
and
The late Sita Ram Goel who blazed a trail of reawakening
and
Shatavadhani Dr R. Ganesh, as always

Contents

Prologue ix
Introduction 1

1 Three Centuries of Imperial Islamic Frustration   9
2 The Turushka Barbarian Barges into the
   Living Room   48
3 The Civilisational Cost of Misplaced Magnanimity   83
4 A Sultanate of Turkic Slaves   104

Bibliography   169
Index   173
About the Author 181

Prologue

The Sultan was ambling his way towards death in one fit of helpless fury at a time. In all probability, the sultan merely suspected that the illness that had seized him this time would pass, too. He was, after all, the Shah, the Upholder of the *Deen*, The Only True Faith in the world, the sultan who had known no defeat, who had 'conquered the east and protect[ed] the west', who had been honoured by none less than the mighty Chief of the Abbasids, and more importantly, he was the One who had 'destroyed the country of the sun-worshippers'.[1] Wherever his sword had been raised, such far-flung, powerful kingdoms like those at Kara[2], Ujjain, Ranthambhor, Chittorgarh, Deogiri[3], Dhur Samundar[4] and Madura[5] met the same fate as that of the 'garden of Behar', whose soil was 'dyed with blood as red as a tulip', and everywhere the ravaging sultan went, the 'Hindus, in alarm, descended into the earth like ants.'[6]

There was really no cause for alarm.

After all, just three years ago, the sultan's realm had witnessed grand regal celebrations on two occasions befitting this grandeur. His eldest son had been married within the family, and then he was declared the sultan's successor. His vassals had dutifully signed on a royal bond signalling their assent. More joy followed. His favourite general and

---

[1] Amir Khusru, "Miftahu-l futuh," in H.M. Elliot and John Dowson, *The History of India as Told by Its Own Historians*, Vol. 3 (London: Trubner & Co, 1871), 543.
[2] Located about 70 km from the city of Prayagraj (formerly Allahabad), it falls in the Kaushambi district.
[3] Devagiri or Daulatabad in Maharashtra.
[4] Dwarasamudra or Halebidu in Karnataka.
[5] Madurai.
[6] Ibid.

intimate consort of at least two decades had brutally crushed the infernal infidel rebel at Deogiri and dispatched a massive booty of elephants, gold and slaves.

It appeared that the sultan's sweeping dominions remained intact and firmly in his iron-like thrall. The succession plan was in place. The rebels were thoroughly vanquished recently. And this accursed illness would be fleeting as before: indeed, what malady would dare touch this Shah destined for explicit immortality?[7]

But something else had also occurred in the last three or four years. The sultan's razor-sharp instinct and innate capacity for near-infallible decision-making had deserted him, a fact that his fast-depleting faculties made him unaware of. His decisions began to culminate in blunders—again, something that he was unaware of. He had fired from service almost all his trusted advisors and officials who had stood unflinchingly by his side throughout his career. When a subversive plot hatched by the wretched neo-Muslims was discovered, he instantly ordered their merciless slaughter: twenty or thirty thousand[8] were massacred in a single day, the majority of them innocent of the plot. His unpopularity soared. His once-formidable court was now completely transformed into a wanton den of debauchery; it had become the butt of jokes, and his vast empire was sitting on a powder keg of ceaseless intrigue among those closest to him. Increasingly, his commands were merely listened to, not obeyed. In those sporadic moments of mental clarity, the sultan, for a fleeting moment, would realize what was happening around him. His favourite queen had at last revealed her true colours, indifferent to his horrible

---

[7] K.S. Lal, *History of the Khaljis* (Allahabad: The Indian Press Ltd, 1950), 311.
[8] A.R. Fuller and A. Khallaque, *The Reign of Alauddin Khilji*, trans. from Zia-ud-din Barani's *Tarikh-i-Firuz Shahi* (Kolkata: Pilgrim Publishers, 1967), 143. See also Lal, *History of the Khaljis*, 296.

suffering. Three years after the pomp, three years too late, he realised that he had appointed a thorough weakling as his successor. And so, as it must, his empire began to splinter and disintegrate, his entire life's work coming apart before his own eyes like a majestic royal brocade slowly coming apart one thread at a time, even as he lay on his imperial bed exhausted and frail and descending slowly into furious insanity.

For succor he turned, as he had always done, to his most loyal Vazir Hazardinari, constantly whining to him about the ingratitude of his queen and his sons and everybody he had nourished and made powerful and prosperous. A sultan whose entire life had been characterised and driven by an insatiable ambition, to attain which he had committed unprecedented savagery backed by religious sanction, had now become a fatalist. And a feeble puppet in the hands of this same Vazir Hazardinari who patiently ministered his every intimate need in that sprawling palace and fort at Siri.

Everybody except the sultan himself knew that he was dying and with him, an extraordinarily savage political career of an unlettered mercenary. A career which had, in a way, begun when he had pulled down a chieftain of Turkish descent from his horse and beheaded him.

But at a fundamental level, the real story of Sultan Ala-ud-din Khalji is simply a continuation of the same trajectory that began approximately in 619. Or nearly ten years after the Prophet Muhammad received his first revelation from the angel Gabriel in the Hira cave on the Jabal an-Nour mountain near Mecca. At the start of this trajectory,

> motivated by the word of God and disciplined by communal prayer, bands of nomadic raiders were transformed into an organized fighting force, whose hunger was now projected outward beyond the desert's rim into a world sharply

divided by faith into two distinct zones. On the one side lay the Dar al-Islam, the House of Islam; on the other, the realms still to be converted, the Dar al-Harb, the House of War.... They besieged cities and learned how to take them. Damascus fell, then Jerusalem itself; Egypt surrendered in 641, Armenia in 653; within twenty years the Persian Empire had collapsed and converted to Islam. The velocity of conquest was staggering.... Finally in 669, within forty years of Muhammad's death, the Caliph Muawiyyah dispatched a huge amphibious force to strike a knockout blow at Constantinople itself.[9]

During the same period, between 636 and 643, this hunger for religion-fuelled imperial conquests also turned its head in the direction of Bharatavarsha or Al-Hind.

Three separate fleets sailed out at various points in time: the first to Thane, the second to Bharuch and the third to Debal.

---

[9] Roger Crowley, *1453: The Holy War for Constantinople and the Clash of Islam and the West* (New York: Hyperion, 2006), 16–17.

Introduction

The Great Mughal is a foreigner in Hindustan. To maintain himself in such a country he is under the necessity of keeping up numerous armies, even in the time of peace.
                                                    François Bernier

In the late 18th century, Tipu Sultan, one of the last Muslim rulers to command a significant kingdom in southern India, wrote frequent, anxious letters to the Caliph, inviting him to invade India and aid him in his fight against the infidel Christians, the British. The underlying significance of all such correspondences is a historical theme that has remained constant from the day the alien invading forces of Islam began their forays into Bharatavarsha, looking for favour, approval and endorsement of their authority in this country from a transnational religious imperialism. With the extinction of the Caliphate in the early years of the 20th century, this religio-imperialist power centre eventually shifted to Saudi Arabia. The most recent, prominent and proximate evidence of this historical phenomenon is the Islamic Republic of Pakistan, which has been consistent in currying favour with and seeking the approval of Saudi Arabia over the last four decades. As the saying goes, the more history changes, the more it remains the same. Sindh, the region where the first Islamic incursions into Bharatavarsha began, wholly belongs to Pakistan today.

> The Mohammedan Conquest of India is probably the bloodiest story in history. It is a discouraging tale, for its evident moral is that civilization is a precarious thing, whose

delicate complex of order and liberty, culture and peace may at any time be overthrown by barbarians invading from without or multiplying within.... The Hindus had allowed their strength to be wasted in internal division and war ... they had failed to organize their forces for the protection of their frontiers and their capitals, their wealth and their freedom, from the hordes of Scythians, Huns, Afghans and Turks hovering about India's boundaries and waiting for national weakness to let them in. For four hundred years ... India invited conquest; and at last it came.[1]

This work deals primarily with some major themes in the political and military history of the period that begins when the conquest mentioned by Will Durant actually came to Bharatavarsha and ends with Babur's invasion of Hindustan, covering the period of the Delhi Sultanate that was in power for three hundred and twenty years. It is spread over five volumes offering a contiguous narrative. However, each volume can also be read as a standalone work.

The Delhi Sultanate period was a time of extraordinary churning that had a far-reaching impact on the history of India that followed it. At many points, it involved critically decisive junctures which had the potential to extinguish—or at any rate, reduce—the severity, dominance and influence of Muslim rule in India. The Delhi Sultanate was endowed with a sort of inbuilt character of ephemerality unlike other Hindu empires that preceded it. In reality, it was strictly not a 'sultanate' in the sense of being an empire ruled continuously by a single dynasty. For instance, for almost a full century after it was established, the Sultanate made no new additions to its territory in mainland India. From 1206 to 1526, it comprised a total of five dynasties, with only one powerful

---
[1] Will Durant, *The Story of Civilization, Volume I: Our Oriental Heritage* (New York: Fine Communications, 1997), 1,004–5.

sultan emerging from each dynasty. Sequentially, these were the Mamluk, Khalji, Tughlaq, Sayyid and Lodi dynasties. Each such 'dynasty' inevitably became extinct within a few years of the death of its most powerful sultan. However, the Delhi Sultanate also heralded several firsts. Hindu kingdoms permanently lost control over almost the entire northwestern part of India. Under Qutub-ud-din Aibak and more emphatically under Shams-ud-din Iltutmish, the fulcrum of political power shifted to Delhi and has more or less remained so till date, although under vastly changed circumstances—a point that this volume discusses. For the first time, Hindus got a full taste of an unbridled military–religious despotism. It was during the Delhi Sultanate regime that the impregnable bastion of the Vindhyas was shattered and southern India experienced the full horrors of an all-out Muslim invasion. It was also a period of all-round sweeping changes: old systems of governance and statecraft were uprooted, the administration was Islamised, an oppressive tax regime was introduced and centuries-old native traditions, worship, manners, customs, dressing, food habits, education and language underwent a brutal and, in many cases, irreversible transformation and destruction. From an overall perspective, it was 320 years of turmoil—at no point in the history of the Delhi Sultanate can we discern a modicum of stability and peace in the real sense, or in the sense that the Indians had known it under, for instance, the regimes similar to that of the Guptas or the Chalukyas. However, this highly volatile rule of the Delhi Sultanate also provided a template which eventually paved the way for the first-ever alien Muslim dynasty to stably rule large parts of Hindustan for a protracted period: the Mughals.

To repeat a widely known fact, Babur's invasion of India marks the fifth decisive milestone in the history of alien Muslim invasions into India. However, both the third *and* the fourth milestones belong to the Delhi Sultanate period.

The third was the defeat of Prithviraja Chahamana or Prithviraj Chauhan in 1192 and the subsequent founding of the Sultanate in 1206 by Qutub-ud-din Aibak. The fourth was the first-ever Muslim ravaging of southern India by Ala-ud-din Khalji in 1296.

All these and other forces of history—to use an overarching term—make this a compelling period. But one of the most important and sadly overlooked factor of the history of this period is narrated in the memorably evocative words of the freedom fighter, fine scholar and prolific author K.M. Munshi, founder of the Bharatiya Vidya Bhavan:

> *The conquests so exultantly referred to by the court chroniclers of the Sultanate had an Indian side of the picture. It was one of ceaseless resistance offered with relentless heroism; of men, from boys in teens to men with one foot in the grave, flinging away their lives for freedom* [emphasis added]; *of warriors defying the invaders from fortresses for months, sometimes for years, in one case, with intermission, for a century; of women in thousands courting fire to save their honour; of children whose bodies were flung into the wells by their parents so that they might escape slavery; of fresh heroes springing up to take the place of the dead and to break the volume and momentum of the onrushing tide of invasion.*[2]

From the time Islam began gaining dominance as a major world religion, historical consciousness became an innate part of the faith, given the fact that the Quran could not be interpreted without a knowledge of history. The conquests of this new ascendant religion had to be recorded in the proper chronological order, with details of treaties, lineages of sultans, names of the heroes of the faith, records of mosques

---

[2] K.M. Munshi, "Foreword," in *The History and Culture of the Indian People*, Vol. 5, ed. R.C. Majumdar (Mumbai: Bharatiya Vidya Bhavan, 2015), xv.

and madrassas erected, gifts made to the clergy and similar details related to the expansion of Islam. Eventually, Muslims became prolific history writers, and Islamic historiography became both a passionate pursuit and a discipline in the community. The ancillary development of this history writing was the exquisite art of calligraphy. Sultans all over the world awarded high official positions and salaries and perks to chroniclers. Thus, we have a continuous, chronological record of the major events of Islamic history in India from the 7th to the 19th century. This includes the history of both Muslim dynasties and various regions in India. However, the basic theme of history writing by these chroniclers remained intact: repeated and vivid glorification of Islam and its conquests and shameless flattery of their patron-sultans. The other side of the coin of this glorification was the appalling venom they poured on the kaffirs or infidels. Two representative samples will suffice here to illustrate this:

> Kutub-ud-din, on whose fortunate forehead the light of world-conquest shone conspicuous ... purged by his sword the land of Hind from the filth of infidelity and vice, and freed the whole of that country from the thorn of God-plurality, and the impurity of idol-worship, and by his royal vigour and intrepidity, left not one temple standing.
> Hasan Nizami

> What is our defence of the faith, cried Sultan Jalaluddin Khalji, that we suffer these Hindus, who are the greatest enemies of God and of the religion of Mustafa, to live in comfort and do not flow streams of their blood?
> Zia-ud-din Barani

The British Civil Service (ICS) officer and historian Vincent A. Smith describes this characteristic of Muslim chroniclers with undisguised distaste.

> [Qutub-ud-din Aibak] was a typical specimen of the ferocious Central Asian warriors of the time, merciless and fanatical. His valour and profuse liberality to his comrades endeared him to the bloodthirsty historian of his age, who praises him as having been a 'beneficent and victorious monarch....' His gifts were bestowed by hundreds of thousands, and his slaughters likewise were by hundreds of thousands. All the leaders in the Muslim conquest of Hindostan similarly rejoice in committing wholesale massacres of Hindu idolaters, armed or unarmed.[3]

But more objectively, Vincent Smith reveals the other side of this story.

> The modern reader of the panegyrics recorded by Muslim authors in praise of 'beneficent' monarchs who slaughtered their hundreds of thousands with delight often longs for an account of their character as it appeared to the friends and countrymen of the victims. But *no voice has come from the grave, and the story of the Muhammadan conquest as seen from the Hindu point of view was never written, except to some extent in Rajputana* [emphasis added].[4]

Against this backdrop, the broad historical narrative of *Invaders and Infidels* that tells the story of both sides, compared and contrasted, is what, I hope, justifies the title of these volumes. From the last century up to our own time, in the abundantly available literature dealing with Muslim histories of India, there is substantial material regarding mostly the Mughal period. However, it appears that works concerning the era of the Delhi Sultanate are few and generally scattered. This is rather surprising given the fact that it was the Delhi

---

[3] Vincent A. Smith, *The Oxford History of India* (Oxford: The Clarendon Press, 1919), 223.
[4] Ibid.

Sultanate that actually primed the field for the Mughals. It is beyond the scope of this introduction to dwell on the reasons for this. One significant reason, however, is the fact that the overall discipline of historical scholarship in India, especially after the 1950s, has largely been destroyed thanks to Marxist ideological manipulation. To put this in real terms, nearly three generations of first-rate scholarship has been wiped out, as a result of which the pioneering work begun by Sir Jadunath Sarkar, R.C. Majumdar, S. Srikanta Sastri, D.C. Sircar, A.D. Pusalker and Radha Kumud Mookerji has continued to languish.

Apart from the primary sources—medieval Muslim chronicles, a few Hindu accounts and inscriptions—the notable works dealing with the history of the Delhi Sultanate are either out of print or are not easily available. While there is no intention to take away from their merit, other works on the subject are written in a fashion not easily accessible to a general reader. For a partial list of these books, see the Bibliography.

Invaders and Infidels is not meant to be an academic work but it draws from and is indebted to a wealth of academic works apart, of course, from various primary and other sources (see Bibliography). The scope of the present work is limited to delineating a broad sweep of largely the political and military dimensions of the history of the Delhi Sultanate. It was an age marked by extraordinary turbulence beginning with Muhammad bin Qasim's invasion of Sindh, whose impact, although devastating in the short run, proved to be enduring in that it opened up possibilities for repeated Islamic invasions of India, first by the Arabs and later, more savagely, by the Turkic Muslims. However, the fact that it took a full five hundred years before a Muslim Sultanate could establish a firm foothold in

Delhi is a story that is narrated more fully in the following pages. This was also a period of extraordinary restlessness, a pivot in the history of the Middle Ages. By 1000, the barbarian Mahmud of Ghazni had savagely proven that Hind was no longer immune from the brutal politics of Central Asia. Iltutmish's efforts at consolidating the fledgling Delhi Sultanate in the early 13th century included a narrow brush with Genghis Khan who had wiped out the Khwarezmian Empire in Persia. And by the middle of the 15th century, even as the other barbarian Timur had ravaged Delhi, Constantinople had fallen to the Ottoman Turks in 1453.

Against this vast and complex canvas of time, geography and forces out of the control of history, these volumes endeavour to present a vigorous narrative having a central theme of events. A general approach has been to describe the chief events and episodes of each period and to provide fuller details based on the importance of the event. Some readers might disagree on some of these points but that only opens up the field for wider and deeper enquiry.

Last but definitely not the least, the vision and approach for writing this series is inspired by the iconic philosopher, poet, author, editor, freedom fighter and multifaceted genius D.V. Gundappa, with whose poignant words I close this introduction:

> History, if it should serve its purpose of stirring emotion, instigating inquiry and directing thought, must first of all be exciting. Is it impossible to be both truthful and warm-hearted, both factual and moving? Are imagination and conscience necessarily enemies to each other? In reconciling them is the art of the true historian. The flow of the story must be swift, vivid, vibrant.[5]

---

[5] D.V. Gundappa, 'The Classical Age', book review broadcast from All India Radio, Mysore, 26 July 1954. Reprinted in *Triveni Journal*, October 1954.

CHAPTER 1

Three Centuries of Imperial Islamic Frustration

Ultimately, after three centuries of unremitting efforts, we find the Arab dominion in India confined to the two petty states of Mansurah and Multan.

R.C. Majumdar

Kulayb 'Little Dog' Abu Muhammad al-Hajjaj was seething. This powerful, ruthless and tenacious governor of the Umayyad Caliphate was smarting from the second consecutive drubbing he had received on the same project of imperial expansion. The reply of admonition that he had just got from the Caliph was an additional blow to his twice-wounded pride.

He was Hajjaj, risen from the shameful embers of debilitating, stone-carrying poverty, derided as a 'little dog' in childhood, mocked for being a lowly schoolteacher. Despite participating in the second fitna, he had received almost no recognition in this most dangerous battle which culminated in establishing the supremacy of the Sunnis in the vast expanse of Arabia. Yet his hour had eventually come. First, the ruthless manner in which he had enforced discipline in the mutinying army of Caliph Abd al-Malik instantly caught the monarch's attention. And then the follow-up: Hajjaj's extraordinary performance in conclusively smashing that accursed rebel Abd Allah al-Zubair, right in the holy city of Mecca where he had holed up defiantly. But Zubair was no ordinary rebel. He was the nephew of Aisha, the most favourite wife of the Prophet himself. Extremely 'pious and chaste, well-versed in the Knowledge of the Quran', Zubair had taken[1] the fire and sword of Islam and delivered terror deep into the heart of *both* the Byzantine and the Sassanid empires. And now he had fallen on truly evil times and was faced with a tragic fate, thanks to those[2] vile Iraqis, 'the worst of any people on the earth'. Hajjaj's victorious march had now arrived at Mecca but he resorted to diplomacy instead of force, obeying the orders of the Caliph who wanted to avoid 'spilling the blood of Muslims' in the city the Prophet had made holy. He gave Zubair three choices, the last of which was to fight until death. Zubair chose the last. For the next seven months, Hajjaj's army besieged and pounded Mecca without respite using

> huge catapults and in it [with] these huge rocks … and they would throw them into Makkah [Mecca] and scores of people would die. On occasions, these would even hit the house of Allah, the Kaaba.[3]

And then Allah himself miraculously intervened

> even as these huge catapults were around Mecca … lightning came from the sky and hit one of these catapults and al Hajjaj ibn Yusuf men were taken aback … this was the blessing of Allah.[4]

---

[1] Muhammad Muhsin Khan, *Sahih Al Bukhari (Arabic–English)*, Vol. 6 (Riyadh: Darussalam Publishers & Distributors, 1997), Book 60, 187.
[2] Sahabah: Companions of the Prophet.
[3] Sheikh Zahir Mahmood, 'The Life of Abd Allah ibn Zubair', Kalamullah.com, accessed 18 February 2020, https://kalamullah.com/zahir-mahmood.html
[4] Ibid.

Hajjaj proclaimed that this was Allah's wrath upon al-Zubair, a proclamation that demoralised the latter's army. Significant defections occurred. Ultimately, in October 692, al-Zubair's leg was chopped off in battle, he was beheaded and his body was mounted on a cross.

Caliph Abd al-Malik was overjoyed, and al-Hajjaj was made governor of Hijaz and Yemen. But he got his real prize in 694 when he was appointed the governor of Iraq. That effectively meant lording over almost half the territory of the Caliphate itself—a vast stretch from Mesopotamia to the ever-expanding territories of Central Asia, which was rapidly falling to the fire and sword of Islam. The bonus was also the fact that the governor directly controlled more than half the income of the Caliphate.

But al-Hajjaj was incredibly hungry. By the early 8th century, he embarked on a massive wave of military expansion that involved industrial-scale genocide, conversions of infidels and the ruthless slaughter of Muslims who dared cross or rebel against him. In his latest zeal for expansion, he commanded three of his most trusted and fearsome generals and dispatched them in three directions. Mujja'a ibn Si'r was entrusted to conquer Oman, Qutayba ibn Muslim to invade Transoxiana[5], and, finally, Muhammad ibn al-Qasim al-Thaqafi to Sindh.

The Indian historical memory is familiar with Muhammad ibn al-Qasim al-Thaqafi simply as Muhammad bin Qasim, the first alien Muslim invader of (undivided) India who located the key that opened the floodgates of nearly a

---

[5] The ancient name given to the region of Central Asia lying between the Amu Darya and Syr Darya rivers. This roughly includes portions of modern-day Uzbekistan, Tajikistan, southern Kyrgyzstan and southwest Kazakhstan.

millennium-long era of unparalleled barbarism, subjugation, religious bigotry and all-encompassing destruction that permanently altered Bharatavarsha. al-Hajjaj held Muhammad bin Qasim in such special esteem that he 'considered him a suitable match for his sister Zaynab'[6]. But there was a deeper, twofold reason for selecting Muhammad bin Qasim for the mission.

The first was rooted in the expansionist zeal of religious–imperialist conquest following the path laid down by the Prophet Muhammad and the unimpeded and seemingly unstoppable march of staggering military successes. From the Byzantine provinces of Egypt, Palestine and Syria to the great Sassanid Empire of Persia and the Turkish-speaking regions of Inner Mongolia, Bukhara and Samarkhand, the armies of Islam had overrun a vast swathe of the earth by 650 by the sheer force of the sword and fire. But these were not merely military conquests.

> Astonishing as these victories of Islamic armies were, equally amazing was the ease and rapidity with which people of different creeds and races were assimilated within the Islamic fold. Syrians, Persians, Berbers, Turks and others – all were rapidly Islamised and their language and culture Arabicised.[7]

In one brutal strike, almost the entire pre-Islamic cultural and civilisational elements of these ancient regions were obliterated forever. And now, these covetous armies looked towards Al-Hind. The second reason al-Hajjaj

---

[6] See "Muḥammad b. al-Ḳasim," in *Encyclopaedia of Islam*, 2nd ed., ed. P. Bearman, et al. (Leiden: Brill, 1960–2005), accessed online on August 2018, https://referenceworks.brillonline.com/entries/encyclopaedia-of-islam-2/*-SIM_5357

[7] Dr Ram Gopal Misra, *Indian Resistance to Muslim Invaders up to 1206 A.D.*, 2nd ed. (Meerut: Anu Books, 1992), 4.

summoned Muhammad bin Qasim was straightforward: retribution.

The early Arab geographers largely recognised the following major 'countries' of Sindh: Kirbun[8], Makran, Al Mand, Kandhir[9], Kasran, Nukan, Kandabil, Armabil, Kanbali, Sahban, Sadusan, Debal, Rasak, Alor, Multan, Sindal, Mandal, Salman, Karaj, Kuli, Kanauj[10] and Baruz[11].

'Think no more of such a design!'

The story really begins years before al-Hajjaj was born. The second Caliph, Umar ibn al-Khattab, appointed Usman as the governor of Bahrain in 636, just four years after Prophet Muhammad's death. The next year, Usman dispatched an army to Thane on the coast of Maharashtra, and for the first time, the hitherto unstoppable Arab armies of Islam had a taste of defeat and humiliation that would recur for nearly three centuries. When the defeated Arab army returned, Usman wrote to Caliph Umar about the failure. An enraged Umar replied:

> O Brother of Sakif ... I swear by God that if our men had been killed, I would have slain an equal number from your tribe.[12]

Next, Usman's brother Hakam dispatched two more expeditions to Al-Hind: to Baruz, modern-day Bharuch in

---

[8] Elliot and Dowson aver that this was a large town in Makran.
[9] Gandhara.
[10] Kanyakubja.
[11] Bharuch. For a fuller description of all these cities and towns, see H.M. Elliot and John Dowson, "Early Arab Geographers," in *The History of India as Told by Its Own Historians*, Vol. 1 (London: Trubner & Co, 1867), 1–94.
[12] Elliot and Dowson, *The History of India as Told by Its Own Historians*, Vol. 1, 116.

Gujarat, and Debal[13], a port near modern-day Karachi. The leader of the Arab army, Mughira, met with some initial success at Debal but was soon killed.

The next Caliph, Uthman ibn Affan[14], in whose regime the Rashidun Caliphate reached its maximum extent of territorial conquest, decided to send a land army to Makran[15], which was part of the kingdom of Sindh. He was advised against the adventure by the governor of Iraq because a messenger who had been sent to survey the area had reported:

> Water is scarce, the fruits are poor, and the robbers are bold; if few troops are sent, they will be slain, if many, they will starve to death.[16]

Uthman's successor Ali ibn Abi Talib, a cousin and son-in-law of Prophet Muhammad, ascended to the Caliphate in 659. One of his generals, Haras ibn Marra-al-Abdi volunteered to attack the same frontier of Sindh hoping that he would succeed where his predecessors had failed. The Caliph sanctioned the expedition. In his first destructive raid in 662, Haras 'was victorious, got plunder, made captives, and distributed a thousand heads in one day'[17]. Emboldened, Haras turned his attention to Kikan (or Kikanan), a small state in the hilly region surrounding

---

[13] There are various accounts about Debal. Its name is said to be a corruption of the Sanskrit word, 'Devalaya'. At any rate, by the time Hakam's forces arrived, Debal was a thriving coastal town, described by early Arab geographers as a 'large mart and the port not only of this but also of the neighbouring regions'. Ibn Haukal describes Debal as famous for manufacturing swords.

[14] Usman.

[15] Makran is now in the Balochistan region forming part of both Iran and Pakistan along the Gulf of Oman.

[16] Elliot and Dowson, *The History of India as Told by Its Own Historians*, Vol. 1, 116.

[17] Ibid.

the Bolan Pass. This time, Haras had outfitted a formidable Muslim army comprising nobles and chiefs. This army encountered no real opposition till it reached the treacherous terrain of Kikan. The state was then a quasi-independent province[18] comprising different pastoral clans hailing from the vigorous Jat community but without any ruling chief. The province was under the direct administration of the king of the so-called 'Brahman' dynasty of Sindh.

The stuff of legends

The Battle of Kikan is truly the stuff of legends. It is on par with, if not more extraordinary, than the fabled Battle of Thermopylae, given the fact that a bunch of pastoral Jats not only outclassed a vastly superior military force—superior in number, training, equipment and war experience—but also inflicted such a crushing defeat that the Caliph took it as a personal humiliation. The *Chachnama* also reports an interesting account of the battle.

> Abdulla bin Sawariya, [was] at the head of four thousand cavalry ... the [Kaikanis] are treacherous, and are protected by their mountain fastnesses from the effects of their rebellion and enmity.... After sustaining a complete defeat from the Kaikanis ... who swarmed around, and closed their egresses by the passes, the remnant of the Arab army returned.[19]

But the portions of this narrative in which the *Chachnama* lapses into silence are filled by the doyen of Indian history, R.C. Majumdar, who assesses this battle in an evocative fashion.

---

[18] R.C. Majumdar (ed.), *The History and Culture of the Indian People*, Vol. 3 (Mumbai: Bharatiya Vidya Bhavan, 2015), 169.
[19] Elliot and Dowson, *The History of India as Told by Its Own Historians*, Vol. 1, 423.

[T]he Bolan Pass was protected by the brave Jats of Kikan or Kikanan. The long-drawn struggles of the Arabs with these powers ... mark their steady but fruitless endeavours to enter India.... The hardy mountaineers of these regions, backed by the natural advantage of their hilly country, offered stubborn resistance to the conquerors of the world, and *though often defeated, ever refused to yield. If there had been a history of India written without prejudices and predilections, the heroic deeds of these brave people, who stemmed the tide of Islam for two centuries, would certainly have received the recognition they so richly deserve* [emphasis added].[20]

Haras himself was killed, and only a handful of his large force scampered back to report the disaster to the Caliph. The casualties on the Jat side were quite significant but the alien invader had been decisively repulsed by a far inferior adversary, a severe psychological blow that the Caliph didn't take lying down. So, for the next twenty years, every successive Caliph made Kikan a special target for conquest and sent as many as six expeditions five of which shattered miserably and 'failed to make any permanent impression'[21] in Sindh. But the Arab Muslims, obstinately, *still* refused to give up. The disgrace was simply too great to endure without wreaking adequate retribution.

Specifically, it was Caliph Mu'awiya ibn Abi Sufyan (or Mu'awiya I) who sent the aforementioned six expeditions, all by land, to Sindh. Five of them were easily repelled with extraordinary slaughter of the Muslim army. The sixth was successful: in 680, Makran finally fell to the Arab Muslims. But it was the failure of the other five that had really worried the Caliph. While the prestige of the Muslims elsewhere in the world grew exponentially with each conquest, these

---

[20] Majumdar, *The History and Culture of the Indian People*, Vol. 3, 174.
[21] Ibid.

THREE CENTURIES OF IMPERIAL ISLAMIC FRUSTRATION 17

serial disasters in a comparatively tiny geographical area of Sindh demanded prudence, not another disaster, not another prestigious injury. Therefore, for the next twenty-eight years, the Arabs did not dare send any army against Sindh.

In the overall reckoning, it was a bleak show right from the first Caliph, Abu Bakr—father of Prophet Muhammad's favourite wife, Aisha—all the way up to Caliph Ali.

The first four pious Caliphs of Islam died without hearing the tidings of even a single victory over Sindh, let alone Al-Hind.

However, al-Hajjaj was not one to give up so easily, especially after tasting spectacular victories elsewhere. Patient and tenacious, he found the perfect opportunity in 708. The pretext: a ship from Serendib (Ceylon) ferrying some Muslim women was captured by pirates near the port of Debal. But these were no ordinary Muslim women. They were special consignment. The 9th-century historian from Baghdad, Ahmad Ibn Yahya al-Baladhuri, narrates the backstory to the incident.

> Ḥajjāj ... appointed Mohammad ibn Harun ibn Zara' al-Namari to rule Mekran [Makran].... Under the government of Mohammad, the king of the Isle of Rubies (Ceylon, so called from the beauty of its women), sent as a present to Hajjaj certain Mohammedan girls who had been born in his country ... but the ship in which he had embarked these girls was attacked and taken by some barks [pirates] belonging to the Meds of Daibul [Debal].[22]

---

[22] Ahmad Ibn Yahya al-Baladhuri, "Futuh-al-Buldan," in Elliot and Dowson, *The History of India as Told by Its Own Historians*, Vol. 1, 118.

al-Hajjaj promptly sent an emissary to Dahir, the Hindu king of Sindh, with the message to set the women free. The undertone of threat was clear. But Dahir, not wishing to be dragged into an unwanted conflict, gently pleaded his inability: he had no authority over the pirates. In many ways, this was the ideal and, perhaps, anticipated response as far as Hajjaj was concerned. He increased the temperature of hostility by demanding a substantial reparation from Dahir. But the response was as before. It was now time for action. Hajjaj wrote a humble submission[23] to the Caliph: vengeance against Dahir's impudence. As bait, Hajjaj offered to pay from his own pocket double the money to compensate what the Caliph would give him for this expedition. In reality, Hajjaj had taken a gamble despite the experience suffered by his predecessors. The gamble had its roots in the fabulous wealth of Sindh which would pay double the amount he had promised. But the Caliph was adamant and mortally scared of any further adventures in Sindh.

> The distance is great, the requisite expenditure will be enormous, and I do not wish to expose the lives of Musulmans to peril.[24]

Eventually, greed triumphed. The Caliph granted permission. To Hajjaj, this mission to Sindh was also crucial owing to a religious reason: more than wreaking vengeance for past defeats, he was determined to subdue a people who had so successfully defied the might of Islam on so many occasions. Hajjaj immediately dispatched 'Ubaidu-lla bin Nabhan to Debal with a sizeable force. However, tragedy struck at Debal. 'Ubaidu-lla was killed in the battle, and his army was thoroughly routed. This setback only made al-Hajjaj

---

[23] Elliot and Dowson, *The History of India as Told by Its Own Historians*, Vol. 1, 431.
[24] Ibid.

more determined. He wrote to another trusted aide, Budail, who was then in Oman. Budail proceeded via sea and was met with reinforcements en route—a three thousand-strong force. At Debal, Jaisimha, the son of Raja Dahir, met Budail and his substantial army. In an intense battle that lasted a full day, the Arab army suffered massive reverses, and towards the end, Budail was thrown off his horse, surrounded by the Hindu army, and his head was chopped off. A good number of Muslim soldiers were taken captive.

But al-Hajjaj remained undaunted as ever. He again wrote to the Caliph requesting permission for yet another expedition. The Caliph wrote back with a rebuke:

> The people of that country are cunning.... It will require unusual skill and might to carry on the war.... This affair will be a source of great anxiety and so we must put it off, for every time an army goes, [vast] numbers of Mussalmans are killed. So think no more of such a design![25]

This time, Hajjaj spoke a mixed dialect: a mixture of Islamic piety, of the rescue of the captured Muslims rotting in the prisons of the infidels, of the burning need for revenge, and of course, of the assured promise of greater riches than before. But this reprimand from the Caliph was the additional blow delivered to the twice-wounded pride of al-Hajjaj, the consequences of whose wrath and fury the inhabitants of his dominions were fully aware of.

Only the hand of Muhammad Bin Qasim...

Astrology can arguably compete with prostitution as the oldest profession in the world. From the soothsayers,

---

[25] Quoted in Sita Ram Goel, *Heroic Hindu Resistance to Muslim Invaders (636 AD to 1206 AD)* (New Delhi: Voice of India, 1994), 2.

charm givers and clairvoyants of untold antiquity right up to Nancy Reagan's astrologer, emperors and monarchs and kings and sultans and members of parliaments and senates have relied on astrology for succour, favour and the promise of power or its reacquisition. It is the eternal industry that is permanently immune to economic downturns.

al-Hajjaj was not immune to astrology.

Sweltering in shame from the serial humiliations and not finding that desperate ray of avenging light, Hajjaj consulted astrologers. Their divination was almost unanimously consistent: the conquest of Sindh could be effected only by the hand of Muhammad bin Qasim.[26] Almost all traditional Muslim historians of Sindh shower lavish praise on Muhammad bin Qasim, hailing from the prestigious Banu Thaqif tribe, as a great warrior and servant of Islam and as someone who took its divine message to the dark corners of Sindh filled with infidels and idolatry and ignorance and other unmentionable religious practices. But there was another significant reason al-Hajjaj chose Qasim to lead the renewed aggression against Sindh. After the miserable and hasty deaths of 'Ubaidu-lla and Budail, and the consequent scolding from the Caliph, Hajjaj realised that he needed to start from scratch. This time, he resolved not to involve himself in any campaign directly. Instead, he carefully handpicked generals[27] who would lead from the front, and for the next four years, he prepared them very carefully, sparing no expense, since he calculated that with victory, he would recover his expenses many times over.

---

[26] "Tuhfatu-l-Kiram," *Chachnama*, Elliot and Dowson, *The History of India as Told by Its Own Historians*, Vol. 1, 432.
[27] See "al-Hadjdjadj b. Yusuf," in *Encyclopaedia of Islam*, accessed on August 2018, https://referenceworks.brillonline.com/entries/encyclopaedia-of-islam-2/al-hadjdjadj-b-yusuf-SIM_2600

As his nephew-cum-son-in-law, Muhammad bin Qasim was the perfect choice. Qasim, in 'the bloom of youth, being only seventeen years of age', was in Fars (now a province in Iran) when his uncle's order arrived sometime in 711–712. The uncle's command, as Qasim set out for Sindh, spat out the fire of brutal determination:

> I swear by Allah that I am determined to spend the whole wealth of Iraq, that is in my possession, on this expedition.[28]

Spain and Sindh

The year 712 marks one of those rare freak but pivotal coincidences in history. In the Western Hemisphere, the young Muslim general Tariq bin Ziyad leading an army of seven thousand troops had inflicted a crushing defeat on and killed the Visigoth chief Roderick and proceeded to conquer most of Spain and Portugal: both these Christian countries offered almost no resistance to the marauding onslaught of the invading Muslim armies. Meanwhile, in faraway Iraq, Muhammad bin Qasim had received blessings to embark on a similar mission to Sindh. It was the initiation of a campaign that unleashed a wanton trail of brutality, bloodshed and a kind of barbarism hitherto unprecedented in the history of Bharatavarsha whose cultural sensibilities couldn't conceive in its wildest dreams that war could even be fought in this fashion.

This time, al-Hajjaj left nothing to chance. He had taken his time to plan everything to the last detail. Muhammad bin Qasim was accompanied by an elite cavalry of six thousand battle-hardened warriors drawn from Syria and Iraq and a matching number of armed camel riders specially trained for arduous and sustained military operations. This was followed

---

[28] Misra, *Indian Resistance to Muslim Invaders up to 1206 A.D.*, 15.

by a luggage train of another three thousand camels from Bactria. Hajjaj's meticulousness can be gauged from the fact that Qasim's retinue included even thread, needles and dressed cotton saturated with strong vinegar, which was then dried in shade. On the matter of the strong vinegar, Hajjaj thought it fit to give valuable dietary advice to his nephew:

> When you arrive in Sind, if you find the vinegar scarce, soak the cotton in water, and with the water you can cook your food and season your dishes as you wish.[29]

Communications was the other element of Hajjaj's diligent planning. Uncle and nephew would exchange correspondence almost on a daily basis throughout Qasim's campaign in Sindh. This would yield highly favourable outcomes for both parties.

The red flag atop the *budd*

When he reached Makran, Qasim was joined by the governor, Muhammad Harun, with more reinforcements: it was a formidable battery of five catapults and assorted ammunition, all of which were then loaded on to ships. Qasim's naval fleet was indeed daunting when we learn the fact that it took about five hundred trained soldiers to work a single catapult. The Fleet of the Faithful commenced its journey towards Debal. There was also a deeply religious reason for using these gigantic catapults: they had been employed by Prophet Muhammad himself in his prolonged siege of Ta'if, which eventually surrendered to him with its inhabitants accepting Islam. So, Qasim was assured that the Prophet's strategy would succeed in Sindh as well. At Debal,

---

[29] Al-Baladhuri, "Futuh al-Buldan," 119.

Abu-l Aswad Jaham, who had been dispatched as the advance guard, joined Qasim.

Outside the fort of Debal, Qasim commanded his men to dig an elaborate trench and appointed spearmen to defend it. Then he installed 'the bride', a *manjanik* or mangonel[30], which took the effort of five hundred battle-hardened strongmen. As he scouted the terrain from his vantage, he spotted a red flag atop a *budd*, a Hindu temple. When the trench work was complete, the siege of Debal had formally begun. Three days later, acting on the instructions of Hajjaj, Qasim ordered the mangonel master to hit the flagstaff. It shattered into pieces at the first impact. Al-Baladhuri recounts what happened next:

> The infidels were sorely afflicted. The idolaters advanced to the combat but were put to flight … the Musulmans escaladed the wall…. The town was thus taken by assault, and the carnage endured for three days. The governor of the town, appointed by Dahir, fled, and the priests of the temple were massacred. Muhammad marked out a place for the Musulmans to dwell in, built a mosque, and left four thousand Musulmans to garrison the place.[31]

This virgin, full-scale assault of the Arab Muslim armies set a pattern which would sickeningly, tragically recur over the next eight hundred years across the length and breadth of India in the aftermath of every Muslim invasion.

When the inhabitants of Nerun (near modern-day Hyderabad in Pakistan) heard that Qasim was proceeding towards them next, they sent two Buddhist priests with an

---

[30] A trebuchet or catapult.
[31] Al-Baladhuri, "Futuh al-Buldan," 120.

appeal for peace no matter what the alien invader demanded in exchange. The tales of bestial horror that had recently occurred at Debal hadn't taken much time to reach their ears. But unlike the bravehearts at Debal who fought to the death, the folks at Nerun had no stomach for resistance. Not only did they meekly capitulate but they also supplied ample provisions to Qasim and offered assistance in his onward campaign. However, there was a backstory to this Buddhist betrayal. R.C. Majumdar gives a more accurate picture of this backstory that greatly aided Muhammad bin Qasim's unimpeded, brutal march of victory:

> The Buddhist priests [in Nerun] were already carrying on treasonable correspondence with Hajjaj, and now openly helped Muhammad with provisions. Muhammad then conquered many cities without any opposition and advanced to Siwistan[32]. Here, too, the Buddhist fifth-columnists welcomed the Arabs and entered into a pact with them against their own governor, who was defeated and fled.[33]

This sort of craven but welcome local support made it relatively easy for Qasim to penetrate deeper into Dahir's territory. When at last he camped on the western bank of the Sindhu (Indus) River, Raja Dahir was truly worried. This was a highly unusual, unforeseen development, which went against his past experiences of easily repelling the *Mleccha*[34] armies on numerous occasions without him lifting a single finger. Qasim had now pitched his tent directly opposite Dahir's army right across the river. Dahir's worry turned to trepidation when he learnt that one of his own subordinate chieftains, Mokah, had deserted him. Mokah's treachery was

---

[32] Modern-day Sehwan Sharif in Pakistan.
[33] Majumdar, *The History and Culture of the Indian People*, Vol. 3, 170.
[34] Foreign; non-Hindu.

also perhaps the first in an infinite train of betrayals of Hindu kings at the most critical hour by those closest to them. While these perfidies were rooted in plain jealousy, avarice and hunger for power, they simultaneously extracted a terrible civilisational cost for Bharatavarsha. Mokah offered to supply boats to Qasim in exchange for a large part of the territory that Qasim had conquered. But it was entirely Dahir's fault for slumbering until this fateful day. He had not bothered to wake up the moment he received intelligence that the upstart Muhammad bin Qasim had amassed such a large force and was proceeding towards his kingdom. The string of easy victories against the Muslim armies in the earlier years had rendered him complacent. But the fall of Debal had essentially sealed Dahir's fate. Al-Baladhuri narrates with considerable pride the tale of the 'dreadful conflict such as had never been heard of'.

> Muhammad and his Musulmans encountered Dahir mounted on his elephant, and surrounded by many of these animals, and his Takukaras [Thakurs] were near his person ... Dahir dismounted and fought valiantly, but he was killed towards the evening, when the idolaters fled, and the Musulmans glutted themselves with massacre. According to Al Madaini, the slayer of Dahir was a man of the tribe of Kalab, who composed some verses upon the occasion.[35]

The *Chachnama*, which also describes the fierce battle in detail, recounts[36] that the site was near Raor[37]. However, on the second day of the battle, the Muslim army was nearly routed because the infidels made a rush on the Arabs from all sides and fought so steadily and bravely that the army of

---

[35] Al-Baladhuri, "Futuh al-Buldan," 122.
[36] Majumdar, *The History and Culture of the Indian People*, Vol. 3, 171.
[37] Near present-day Nawabshah, Benazirabad district, Pakistan.

Islam became irresolute and their lines were broken up in great confusion.

After Dahir was killed, his son, the same Jaisimha who had inflicted a crushing defeat on Arab armies earlier, now retreated to Brahmanabad[38]. It was left to the widowed queen of Dahir to defend the fort of Raor against Qasim's army, which had tasted the fresh blood of a major victory and was thirsty for more. This valiant lady offered extraordinary resistance and when she realised that the inevitable was staring at her, that she couldn't defend the fort any longer, she made the ultimate decision. She had heard enough stories about the appalling horrors that women captured by victorious Muslim armies underwent. She didn't want to verify the truth of those stories by personally experiencing them. With her action, she had also inaugurated what later became a recurrent feature among Hindu women whose kingdom had been defeated by Muslim armies: Jauhar. Her spunky address to the ladies in the fort is worth recounting:

> Jaisimha is separated from us and Muhammad Qasim is at the gates. God forbid that we should owe our liberty to these outcast cow-eaters! Our honour would be lost! Our respite is at an end, and there is nowhere any hope of escape; let us collect wood, cotton, and oil, for I think that we should burn ourselves and go to meet our husbands. If any wish to save herself she may.[39]

The womenfolk heeded her call and followed her into a room in the fort and set it on fire, with themselves as the sacrificial fodder.

---

[38] Present-day Mansura in Pakistan.
[39] *Chachnama*, in *The History of India as Told by Its Own Historians*, Vol. 1, 172.

Muhammad bin Qasim stormed the fort and in a space of two or three days, massacred six thousand soldiers and took the non-combatants and their dependents, wives and children as slaves. The number totalled up to thirty thousand. The kind of wealth he witnessed there was beyond even the realm of his comprehension. According to the pious custom laid down by the Prophet himself, Qasim judiciously divided the war spoils. One-fifth of the booty was sent to al-Hajjaj. Apart from gold and other precious pickings, this included the infidel war prisoners who became slaves, another first in the annals of the history of Bharatavarsha. The slain Dahir's head was also part of these spoils of war. When it arrived, al-Hajjaj was ecstatic. He prostrated himself on the ground and prayed to Allah, offering Him thanksgiving and said, 'I have in reality obtained all the wealth and treasures and dominions of the world'[40]. After this, he promptly forwarded a portion of his war spoils to the Caliph along with Dahir's head. Hajjaj had indeed fulfilled the promise he had made to the Caliph. But little did he know that more bounty would be coming his way.

Meanwhile, Jaisimha had erected elaborate defences both at Brahmanabad and his capital city, Alor. Unlike his father Dahir, Jaisimha decided to launch an offensive. And so, when Muhammad bin Qasim reached Brahmanabad, he encountered a vigorous pushback. Jaisimha cut off Qasim's supplies and harassed him repeatedly using a variety of tactics. Tragically, as with his father, Jaisimha's wazir (chief minister) defected to the enemy camp. Despite this reversal, Jaisimha continued the brave fight for six long months. Ultimately, greater numbers of people in his inner circle betrayed the

---

[40] Ibid., 173.

fort of Brahmanabad, at which point Jaisimha was forced to flee. Muhammad bin Qasim's rage was boundless. According to Al-Baladhuri, Qasim slaughtered as many as twenty-six thousand people in the place. Other Muslim historians[41] estimate the figure at eight thousand. Soon, even the capital Alor fell to Qasim. In both places, he built a mosque, erected a Muslim garrison and stationed a prefect.

When Mulastana became Multan

Mulastana—the original name of the Islamicised 'Multan'—is a great city hailing from untold antiquity. The general region has been continuously inhabited for over five thousand years and is one of the proverbial cradles of human civilisation, now home to numerous archaeological sites dating back to the early Harappan period of the Indus Valley Civilisation. According to Hindu lore, Mulastana was founded by Rishi Kashyapa and was the capital of the Trigarta kingdom when the Great Kurukshetra War occurred. During Alexander's raid of India, Mulastana was located on an island in the Ravi River (known as Iravati or Parushni in Vedic texts). This ancient city is now fabled for a proliferation of mosques, minarets and a vast collection of Islamic structures. It is also home to the largest collection of Sufi shrines in a single place.

However, for at least three thousand years, Mulastana was one of the original homes that embodied and breathed the sanctity of the *Sanatana* Vedic civilisation and culture, which found its most magnificent and sublime expression in the Aditya (or Sun) Temple. According to the *Bhagavata Purana*, it was built by Krishna's son Samba who performed a penance to propitiate Aditya in order to obtain a cure for his leprosy. When Chinese traveller Hiuen Tsang visited the

---
[41] Ibid., 122.

Sun Temple in 641, he described the *murti* of Aditya as made of 'pure gold with eyes made from large red rubies'. Its doors, pillars and the *shikhara* (tower/dome) were all studded with silver, gold, rubies, gems and numerous varieties of precious metals. At a more profound level, Mulastana was one of the most sacred pilgrimage centres for Hindus, on par with Kashi, Prayagraj, Mathura and Kanchipuram.

Quite naturally, the profusion of tales of its splendid grandeur and wealth that Muhammad bin Qasim heard about heightened his thirst for plunder and evoked the same religious piety that he had displayed at Debal, Alor and elsewhere. When his army arrived in the precincts of Mulastana after crossing the Beas River and declared war, the Hindus fought back with solid grit. But then, the frontier guard of Mulastana was badly outnumbered against the invader's army; those who managed to survive fled into the town. Its gates were locked tightly shut. The Hindus had taken extreme care to safeguard their sacred city. Mulastana was impregnable. Almost. Muhammad bin Qasim realised too, that Mulastana wouldn't capitulate so easily. But owing to his unstoppable victorious march ever since he set foot in India, he was determined to take the city at any cost. The loot that he had amassed at Debal, Raor and other places paled in comparison to these descriptions he had heard about the city's extraordinary opulence. Meanwhile, his experiences so far had taught him several valuable lessons regarding the political configuration in Sindh and the character, moral values and religious beliefs of the idolaters. He hoped to put that knowledge to good use in his ongoing siege of Mulastana, which lasted for two months—at the end of which his provisions had been completely exhausted, to the disgraceful extent that the 'Musulmans were reduced to eating donkeys.'[42]

---

[42] Ibid.

Once again, Hindu betrayal favoured him. An unnamed citizen of Mulastana revealed a vital secret to Qasim in exchange for pecuniary and other benefits. The secret to Mulastana's prolonged and enduring defence was the aqueduct that supplied drinking water to the entire town from the Basmad River. Muhammad bin Qasim wasted no time in destroying the entire water course. Left with no other option, the inhabitants offered conditional surrender to Muhammad bin Qasim: their sacred Aditya Temple was not to be harmed in any manner. Qasim agreed. Al-Baladhuri vividly narrates what happened after Qasim's army entered Mulastana:

> Muhammad bin Qasim massacred the men capable of bearing arms, but the children were taken captive, as well as the Purohits of the temple, to the number of six thousand. The Musulmans found there much gold in a chamber ten cubits long by eight broad, and there was an aperture above, through which the gold was poured into the chamber. Hence they call Multan 'the Frontier of the House of Gold,' for farj means 'a frontier.' The Budd (temple) of Multan received rich presents and offerings, and to it the people of Sind resorted as a place of pilgrimage. They circumambulated it, and shaved their heads and beards. They conceived that the image was that of the prophet Job—God's peace be on him![43]

Muhammad bin Qasim plundered the entire wealth of the grand Aditya Temple of Mulastana and as before, sent the spoils to his master and father-in-law, al-Hajjaj, who was overjoyed at this substantial bounty. He made a rough calculation. He had spent a whopping sixty million dirhams fitting out Muhammad bin Qasim's expedition. What he had now received was exactly double the sum, a news which made him exclaim again:

---

[43] Ibid,123.

We have appeased our anger, and avenged our injuries, and we have gained sixty millions of dirhams, as well as the head of Dahir.[44]

As before, Qasim built a mosque in Multan before departing from the ancient sacred Vedic city renowned for high culture and spirituality, which he had overnight reduced to a smouldering and bloody ruin. The Arabic historians mention—vastly different from what Hiuen Tsang records—that the *murti* was made from wood (akin to what we find in the Jagannath Temple at Puri) covered with a red skin and 'adorned with two rubies for eyes'. In a shrewd act of foresight, Muhammad bin Qasim did not destroy it. The subsequent Muslim invaders and chieftains who ruled Multan followed Qasim's lead: the wealthy and substantial offerings that Hindu pilgrims made to this deity on a daily basis were confiscated[45] from the temple management and added to the royal treasury until[46] Jalam bin Shayban, the leader of the Ismaili Shia Qarmatians broke it, slaughtered the Brahmin purohits en masse and converted the grand Aditya Temple into a Jami Masjid in the mid-10th century.

---

[44] Ibid., 123.
[45] Al-Biruni provides a graphic account of the fate of the main *murti* inside the sanctum sanctorum of the Aditya Temple when Multan was invaded by one Muhammad Ibn Alkasim Ibn Almunaibh: 'A famous idol of theirs was that of Multan, dedicated to the sun, and therefore called Aditya. It was of wood and covered with red Cordovan leather; in its two eyes were two red rubies. It is said to have been made in the last Kritayuga. When Muhammad Ibn Alkasim Ibn Almunaibh conquered Multan, he inquired how the town had become so very flourishing and so many treasures had there been accumulated, and then he found out that this idol was the cause, for there came pilgrims from all sides to visit it. Therefore, he thought it best to have the idol where it was, but he hung a piece of cow's flesh on its neck by way of mockery. On the same place a mosque was built.' — Edward C. Sachau, *Alberuni's India*, Vol. 1 (London: Kegan Paul, Trench, Trubner & Co, 1910), 116.
[46] Mumtaz Ali Tajddin, *Encyclopaedia of Ismailism* (Karachi: Islamic Book Publisher, 2006).

Before Muhammad bin Qasim left Multan, he faithfully implemented the orders he received in a letter from Hajjaj:

> Wherever there is an ancient place or famous town or city, mosques and pulpits should be erected there; and the Kutba should be read, and the coin struck in the name of this [Caliph's] government. And as you have accomplished so much with this army by your good fortune ... be assured that to whatever place of the infidels you proceed it shall be conquered.[47]

Accordingly, Qasim erected a massive Jama Masjid and some minarets, thus planting the victorious flag of Islam in Multan. The original Mulastana was largely a thing of the past.

As a cruel footnote to the barbaric history of the tragedy the Aditya Temple suffered, its ruins today[48] lie next to the grave of the unvarnished Sunni and Sufi bigot and poet, Bahauddin Zakariya, a spiritual advisor to Iltutmish.

With the death of al-Hajjaj in 714, and the succession of Caliph Al-Walid, Muhammad bin Qasim's fate was sealed.

---

[47] Elliot and Dowson, *History of India as Told by Its own Historians*, Vol. 1, 206–207.
[48] Here is how a privately funded sacred-heritage preservation group in Pakistan describes the current state of the Aditya Temple: 'The Sun Temple now only exists in ruins, overshadowed by the well-preserved Muslim sites located in its vicinity. Evidence of the presence of an ancient grand temple at this location now only exists in history books. A centuries-old place of worship, that has been praised in several historical narratives, now exists as a ghost of the past, overlooked and completely neglected by the authorities and public alike. The site where the grand temple once existed now suffers from encroachment. It is put to use very rarely, for the purpose of pitching tents for the Muslim pilgrims that come to Multan for the Urs (death anniversary) of the saints in the surrounding shrines. Major portions of the temple have been demolished, the roof the temple has caved in, all the idols are gone, and nothing indicates presence of a majestic spiritual site that once existed here in all its glory. The centuries-old Sun Temple has been forever lost to posterity. ' — Sara Akhlaq, 'The Other Heritage: Hindu Temples of Pakistan', accessed on December 2019, https://www.sacredfootsteps.org/2019/11/15/the-other-heritage-hindu-temples-of-pakistan

In keeping with the Islamic political tradition of finishing off enemies to the last man, woman and child, Walid imprisoned and killed al-Hajjaj's family members. However, Walid himself died within a year and was succeeded by his brother Sulayman who immediately dismissed all appointees of Hajjaj. Muhammad bin Qasim was dismissed as the governor of Sindh and recalled. Upon return, he was captured and fettered like an ordinary criminal and then imprisoned and slowly tortured to death[49] in Wasit in eastern Iraq, meeting a truly gory end. The same Muhammad bin Qasim who inflicted such brutal horrors for over three years in India died worse than a common criminal. His pious services towards advancing the Only True Faith in a land full of infidels were not even acknowledged, a fact that reveals the real nature of Islamic imperialism throughout its history.

Opening the gates

For the first time in its history, Muhammad bin Qasim gave Bharatavarsha a taste of what an Islamic invasion really symbolised and how it played out on the ground. Hindus could not, even in the wildest stretch of their imagination, conceive of a war that defied description. Until then, the code of war ethics that they had inherited since the Vedic period rested upon a rather tempered, three-tiered categorisation, given, for example, by Kalidasa[50], which was later elucidated by the Kashmiri scholar, Vallabhadeva. The first was a Dharmavijayi[51], which refers to a conqueror who after defeating his enemy, allows him to rule the

---

[49] The *Chachnama* contains a fictional romantic tale about the revenge wreaked upon Muhammad bin Qasim by two daughters of Dahir who had been captured and sent to the Caliph's harem.
[50] See M.R. Kale, *Raghuvamsha of Kalidasa* (Bombay: Gopal Narayen & Co, 1922).
[51] A conqueror who attains military victory by waging war according to rules laid down by Dharma.

territory as before but exerts administrative control over him. The second was a Lobhavijayi[52]—a conqueror who, after defeating his enemy, snatches both his territory and his treasury but spares the defeated king's life. And the third was an Asuravijayi[53]—a conqueror who not only grabs his vanquished enemy's territory and treasury but puts him to death and takes his entire family, including women and children, as slaves. Needless to say, the Hindu tradition holds the Asuravijayi as the most despicable form of military victory. But the kind of war that Muhammad bin Qasim waged went beyond the pale of even an Asuravijayi. It is also significant that Vallabhadeva, writing in the 10th century, felt the need to expound in detail on these three gradations of military victories in a Sanskrit commentary on Kalidasa's poetic work, *Raghuvamsha*. By the 10th century, Kashmir had already faced repeated attempts at total Islamic conquest. The crushing defeat inflicted by Lalitaditya Muktapida on the Arab raider Junaid in the mid-8th century, and later, the failure of another raider Hisham ibn 'Amr al-Taghlibi were little consolations in hindsight, because the Hindu rulers of Kashmir (and elsewhere) had failed to understand the exact nature of the beast they were facing. And so when the arch barbarian Mahmud of Ghazni surged into Kashmir with a large army in 1002, the Hindu king there was no match for him. Although large-scale Islamisation of Kashmiri Hindus occurred only in the 14th century, the raids of Mahmud had done significant damage. In this backdrop, it was perhaps Vallabhadeva's attempt to remind and reawaken his Hindu brethren to their own glorious and

---

[52] A conqueror who attains military victory by waging war by significantly violating the rules laid down by Dharma.

[53] A conqueror who attains military victory by waging war completely bereft of any principle.

noble martial traditions that were facing a mortal threat from the marauders from Arabia.

There were Two other crucial factors that contributed to the success of Muhammad bin Qasim. When they heard of Qasim's triumphs in the 'accursed infidel lands of Hind', which had repeatedly repulsed the warriors of Islam, substantial numbers of adventurers, plunderers and freelance mercenaries from faraway Damascus journeyed to Hind, 'eager for plunder and proselytism'[54]. When Qasim left towards Dipalpur after razing Mulastana, his force had swelled to a massive fifty thousand. This number[55] does *not* include the chieftains and prefects and contingents of Muslims he had left behind in the areas he had conquered. The second factor is the military assistance provided to Qasim by a disgruntled section of the Jat and Med[56] warriors. They joined his army in a fit of rage against their ill treatment by their former Hindu rulers at Brahmanabad. H.M. Elliot and John Dowson offer an interesting observation of this psyche:

> [T]he Jats and Meds enlisting under ... Kasim's banners, which, *independent of its moral effect in dividing national sympathies,* and relaxing the [unity] of defence against foreign aggression, *must have been of incalculable benefit to him* ... the [mistreatment] of [Jats and Meds] *were more suited to Musalman intolerance than the mild sway of Hinduism* ... accordingly, after the conqueror's first acquisitions, we

---

[54] Elliot and Dowson, *The History of India as Told by Its Own Historians,* Vol. 1, 435.
[55] "Tarikh-i Sind", "Tuhfatu-l Kiram", quoted in Ibid.
[56] Meds are perhaps the oldest inhabitants of the Sindh, Punjab and Haryana regions who traced their ancestry to the Mahabharata. They were a pastoral tribe who gradually became warriors. The early Arab geographers and chroniclers note the ceaseless hostility between Jats and Meds.

find him so indifferent about retaining the good will of his allies, that *he imposed the same conditions upon them, which he enforced with even greater stringency than his predecessors* [emphases added].[57]

If Muhammad bin Qasim was the herald of an unparalleled savage precedent of an imperial raid that had religious sanction, he also ironically heralded another precedent on the Hindu side: betrayal and shortsighted compromises with a determined and fanatical alien enemy which extracted enormous civilisational costs from the Hindus. This phenomenon would recur uncountable times for about a millennium, a period that includes numerous episodes of sabotage of the Indian freedom movement by Indians themselves.

The revenge of Jaisimha

However, Muhammad bin Qasim's fabled success in Sindh was just the proverbial flash in the pan. It was as though the people of the territories he had conquered were waiting for his departure. The selfsame Dahir's son Jaisimha immediately reoccupied Brahmanabad and Alor and grew from strength to strength. Likewise, other chiefs of Sindh cast off the Muslim yoke that had been imposed on them and regained their former power.

When Caliph Umar II noticed this, he sent a force that managed to subdue a few chiefs but the Caliph realised that there was no way he could impose a permanent occupation in these regions without substantial losses. So he offered a choice to leave them independent on the condition of accepting Islam. Some Hindu chiefs, including Jaisimha, agreed. But he quickly reverted to Hinduism under the

---

[57] Ibid.

Caliphate of Hisham and declared war against Junaid, the governor of Sindh. Unfortunately, he lost and became Junaid's prisoner. The Hindu royal dynasty of Sindh was permanently finished with Jaisimha as its last tragic hero who submitted to Islam as a matter of strategy but refused to succumb to the alien invader till the very end.

'A place of refuge to which the Muslims might flee was not to be found'

But Muhammad bin Qasim had also set another precedent: he had shown that Sindh could indeed be breached and conquered with skilful strategy and extraordinary planning. Successive Caliphs did make repeated attempts, all of which failed. Whatever little conquests the Arab Muslim armies had made in Sindh had all failed to endure. The Hindu population was too proud of its heritage and had unshakeable confidence in its civilisational strength to meekly accept this alien barbarism. They rebelled, killed or chased out the foreigner at the first opportunity they got.

This recurrent feature of the early-medieval period in Indian history can accurately be called the Imperial Islamic Frustration of Three Centuries.

The chain of events that began with the proud Jaisimha would confront the Arab Muslims like a regular nightmare endowed with an endless power of reincarnation. Between 724 and 738, Junaid, aided by his lieutenants, overran an impressive swathe of territory, including Jaisalmer, parts of Jodhpur, Bharuch, Navsari, Barmer (or Vallabhamandala), Malwa and Ujjain. He was largely successful because these regions were ruled by major and minor chieftains who were thoroughly unprepared and hopelessly disunited. But when the Arab armies met the Pratihara king Nagabhata and the Chalukya king Avanijanashraya[58] Pulikeshi, they were thoroughly beaten, suffering severe losses. As a mark of this victory, Pulikeshi earned grand titles, like 'the solid pillar of South India'[59] and 'repeller of the unrepellable'[60]. The fate of the invading forces was even worse in the north, where the Kashmiri king Lalitaditya Muktapida, in alliance with Kanauj's king Yashovarman, inflicted extraordinary humiliation on the Arab armies. Lalitaditya ordered the *Mlecchas* to shave off half their heads as a symbol of their submission. Further, under Junaid's successor Tamin, the Arab Muslims lost all the newly conquered territories and had to flee and seek shelter in the selfsame Sindh, which Muhammad bin Qasim had so successfully conquered. But even here, their position became dangerously untenable. They hurriedly built a new city on an isolated side of the lake bordering Hind. The city was akin to a shelter, which protected them from the accursed infidels. A measure of the mortal fear that the Hindus had instilled in the Arabs can be gauged from this lament by the Arab chronicler Al-Baladhuri:

> The Musulmans have retired from several parts of India and abandoned some of their positions; nor have they up to the present advanced so far as in days gone by ... The people of Hind returned to idolatry with the exception of the inhabitants of Qasbah. *A place of refuge to which the Muslims might flee was not to be found* [emphasis added], so he [the Arab governor] built on the further side of the lake, where it borders on Al-Hind, a city which he named Mahfuzah [the protected] establishing it as a place of refuge for them, where they should be secure...[61]

---

[58] Literally, Refuge and Protector of the People of Mother Earth.
[59] 'Dakshinapatha-sadhata'.
[60] 'Anivarttaka-nivartayi'.
[61] Majumdar, *The History and Culture of the Indian People*, Vol. 3, 173. See also Misra, *Indian Resistance to Muslim Invaders up to 1206 A.D.*, 420.

By the end of the 8th century, the might and prestige of Islam which had reached untrammelled heights of triumph across a vast geography that sliced across the Middle East, North Africa, Portugal and Spain and was knocking on the doors of France, had reached its nadir in Al-Hind. That this ebb of Islamic power also coincided with the decimation of the Umayyad Caliphate at the hands of the Abbasid Caliphate is noteworthy as we shall see later in this book.

By the 10th century, Arab travellers to India record, only two tiny, independent Arab principalities existed in all of Al-Hind: Multan and Mansurah. Multan was especially vulnerable. The Pratihara kings waged an unremitting war against the Arab ruler to wrest the ancient, sacred city back into the Hindu fold. However, it was the selfsame Aditya *Budd* that ironically saved the Arab ruler. The account of the 10th-century Arab traveller-chronicler-geographer al-Istakhri is telling:

> Multan is a city about half the size of Mansurah. There is an idol there held in great veneration by the Hindus, and every year people from the most distant parts undertake pilgrimages to it, and bring to it vast sums of money, which they expend upon the temple and on those who lead a life of devotion in that city. The temple of the idol has a strong ... edifice, situated in the most populous part of the city, in the market of Multan, between the bazar of the ivory dealers and the shops of the coppersmiths.... When the Indians make war upon [Multan] and endeavour to seize the idol, *the* [Musulmans] *bring it out, pretending that they will break it and burn it. Upon this the infidels retire, otherwise they would destroy Multan* [emphasis added].[62]

---

[62] Al-Istakhri, "Kita'bu-l Aka'lim", quoted in *The History of India as Told by Its Own Historians*, Vol. 1, 28.

The late historian Dr Ram Gopal Misra makes the following blunt but honest observation about this state of affairs at Multan:

> Thus after three centuries of unremitting effort, we find the Arab dominion in India limited to two petty states of Multan and Mansurah. And here, too, *they could exist only after renouncing their iconoclastic zeal and utilizing the idols for their own political ends. It is a very strange sight to see them seeking shelter behind the very budds they came here to destroy* [emphasis added].[63]

The so-called Arab invasion of Sindh was a monumental debacle. After three centuries of unceasing effort and enormous investment in men and money, the outcome was fabulously pathetic. Even in Multan and Mansurah, the real nature of the Arab occupation was temporary, hesitant, insecure and vulnerable. It was a feeble forerunner to and not the inception of Muslim rule in Bharatavarsha.

The chief reason for the repeated pounding that the Arab Muslim armies received in India owes to the incredibly sturdy and enduring foundations of the *Sanatana* Dharmic state and military organisation that sustained the might of Hindu kingdoms. This well-oiled military organisational superstructure[64], with its subterranean links of loyal coordination down to the last village headman who was responsible for maintaining his own army, was a direct inheritance from the time of Chandragupta Maurya. This brilliant and farsighted vision emanating from the genius of Chanakya Kautilya was wisely and vigorously retained,

---

[63] Misra, *Indian Resistance to Muslim Invaders up to 1206 A.D.*, 21.
[64] See, for example, Jadunath Sarkar, *Military History of India* (Kolkata: M.C. Sarkar & Sons Pvt Ltd, 1960); Uma Prasad Thapliyal, *Warfare in Ancient India: Organizational and Operational Dimensions* (New Delhi: Manohar Publishers, 2010).

THREE CENTURIES OF IMPERIAL ISLAMIC FRUSTRATION 41

expanded and greatly improved by the Gupta Empire. In turn, the successors of the Gupta empire, too, preserved the same. This significant but overlooked fact of Indian history becomes clearer when we contrast it with most other nations that encountered the armies of Islam during that period. It was the same story everywhere: large-scale massacres of Christians and other non-Muslims, industrial-scale plunder, mass conversions to Islam, slave-taking, desecrations of their religious places, and enforcing the *zimmi* (or *dhimmi*) status to non-Muslims whose numbers were too great to slaughter.

Bharatavarsha was the only exception. For a pragmatic reason.

Elliot and Dowson observe that in the aftermath of Muhammad bin Qasim's destructive raids at Debal, Alor and Multan, the

> toleration which the native [Hindus] enjoyed in the practice of their religion was greater than what was usually conceded in other countries; *but it was dictated less by any principle of justice or humanity, than the impossibility of suppressing the native religion by the small number of Arab invaders* [emphasis added].[65]

However,

> Where power had, for a short time, enabled the Moslims to usurp the mastery, *the usual bigotry and cruelty were displayed.* At Debal, the temples were demolished, and mosques founded; a general massacre endured for three whole days; prisoners wore taken captive; plunder was amassed.... At Nairun, the idols were broken, and mosques founded, notwithstanding its

---

[65] Elliot and Dowson, *The History of India as Told by Its Own Historians*, Vol. 1, 468–9.

> *voluntary surrender ... the temples were treated like 'churches of the Christians, or synagogues of the Jews...'* [emphasis added][66]

In Damascus, which fell in 634 and Jerusalem, in 637, the situation was truly horrific. The ringing of bells was prohibited in churches and constructing new chapels was strictly forbidden. Muslims had unrestricted access at all times to churches and synagogues. In fact, 'free admission of Musulmans to these places was at all times compulsory.'[67] Churches were forcibly converted into mosques without any compensation and some of them were intentionally converted into cattle sheds, stables and slaughterhouses.

None of this was imposed on the Hindus of Debal and Multan due to sheer political expediency and the unstable nature of the raid. However, where opportunity afforded itself, the alien Arabian settlers did the best within their limited means to harass the infidel Hindus. There was a fundamental reason for this relaxation in the strict Islamic code regarding the treatment of non-Muslims:

> In Central Asia, the idolaters had been rooted out. But this experiment failed in Sind as Islam was confronted with a faith which, though idolatrous, defied death and looked at life in this world as one link in the eternal chain of births and deaths.[68]

One of the most original historical scholars of the last century, Sita Ram Goel sheds further light on this.

> [T]he apologists for Islamism have presented this expediency as a proof of Islamic liberalism under the early Arabs. They have contrasted this Arab liberalism with the fanaticism of

---

[66] Ibid.
[67] Ibid.
[68] Misra, *Indian Resistance to Muslim Invaders up to 1206 A.D.*, 22.

THREE CENTURIES OF IMPERIAL ISLAMIC FRUSTRATION   43

the Turks who joined the fold of Islam at a later stage.... The mullahs and sufis of Islam might have howled over this dilution of the dogma. But the military and political leaders always knew when and where to make a compromise in the interests of self-preservation...[69]

However, unlike any of the earlier alien raids into India beginning with Alexander and then the Kushans, Muhammad bin Qasim's brutal storming of Sindh was highly unusual in character for a unique reason—it left a permanent legacy of political and social turmoil in India because his aims and methods were continued by successive Muslim raiders and conquerors even after they had permanently settled in India and become rulers and founded empires. For the first time, defenceless people—men, women and children—were captured en masse as slaves for lifelong servitude and trade in the lucrative slave markets of the Middle East. It took a significantly long period for Hindus to come to terms with this brutal fact of Muslim conquest and rule.

Classical Hindu era decimated

The Imperial Islamic Frustration of Three Centuries would soon begin to thaw. Tenth-century India saw a period of frenzied political activity during which the country resembled a warring and bloody playground of Hindu kingdoms cutting each other's throats for territory. By all accounts, it is a remarkable and decisive century that permanently altered the course of India's history. It witnessed the demise of three vast and major empires—the Rashtrakutas in the south, the Palas in the east and the Pratiharas in the west and north. At various points, all three were busy dealing death blows to one another, oblivious to the quiet stirrings of a catastrophe

---
[69] Goel, Heroic *Hindu Resistance to Muslim Invaders (636 AD to 1206 AD)*, 4.

silently lurking in Sindh. But that would come a little later. At the end of the 10th century, the theatre of history was slowly unfolding in faraway Kabul. Actually, the curtains had been slowly but decisively raised about a century ago.

In 870, Yaqub bin Layth, a Turkish coppersmith, mercenary and adventurer from Seistan[70], who began his career as the chief of a band of brigands, quickly attracted the attention of the Abbasid Caliphate for his successful exploits against their sworn enemies, the Kharijites, who had dared to rebel against the authority of the Caliphate. He rose through the ranks meteorically and became the founder[71] of what came to be known as the (short-lived) Saffarid dynasty. With an eye on Al-Hind, he sent a honeyed message to the ruler of Kabul and literally stabbed him in the back with a lance when the two met. His Turkish army then invaded the Hindu kingdoms of Kabul and Zabul. The fate of Zabul was particularly gruesome: after its king was killed in the battle, its entire population was converted to Islam by force. However, this was still a mere eclipse that had engulfed Kabul. After the death of Yaqub bin Layth in 879, the Hindu king Lalliya Shahi (Kallar) who had shifted his capital to Udbhandapur returned and quickly reconquered Kabul. However, by then, Kabul had permanently lost its original Hindu character. The Arab traveller-geographer-chronicler al-Istakhri gives the following picture of Kabul in 921.

> *Kábul has a castle celebrated for its strength, accessible only by one road. In it there are Musulmáns, and it has a town, in which are infidels from Hind [Emphasis added].*[72]

---

[70] Modern-day Sistan in Pakistan.

[71] See "Yaqub bin Layth," in *Encyclopædia Iranica*, online edition, accessed on 20 September 2016, http://www.iranicaonline.org/articles/yaqub-b-lay-b-moaddal

[72] Sir H.M. Elliot, *The Hindu Kings of Kabul* (London: Packard Humanities Institute, 1869), 3.

In 963, with Ghazna (or Ghazni) in eastern-central Afghanistan as his base, Alp-Tigin[73], a Turkish slave commander of the Samanid dynasty, succeeded in establishing an independent Muslim principality in Kabul. However, it was originally his daring capture of Ghazni that truly changed the fortunes of mainland India for the worse.

Ghazni, meaning 'jewel', is located on a plateau and is sandwiched between Kandhahar (or Gandhara) and Kabul. For thousands of years, it served as the main road connecting Kabul and southern Afghanistan and remains a highly strategic city. It was originally founded as a small market town and is perhaps one of the few antiquarian cities which had the misfortune of being kicked around like a football: from the Achaemenid king Cyrus II to Alexander to the Saffarids to the Ghaznavids to the Ghurids to the Mughals to Nadir Shah to the Durranis to the British and finally, to the Taliban. Perhaps no other ancient city has been repeatedly destroyed so spectacularly with sickening regularity. Till this day, Ghazni retains its pre-eminence as the key to the possession of Kabul.

Alp-Tigin's capture of Ghazni received formal recognition from the Samanids. He was now the official governor of Ghazni, a title that would eventually pave the way for sweeping, barbaric and history-altering changes. However, Alp-Tigin didn't live long to savour the fruits of his conquest. He died just a few months later, in September 963. His slave, son-in-law and general, 'beloved prince' Abu Mansur Sabuktigin succeeded him in 977, after a period marked by weak successors and the misrule of Pirai, another slave of Alp-Tigin. Pirai was expelled from the governorship and Sabuktigin took his place in 977. However, that was just the beginning of his troubles. Pirai's misrule was the

---

[73] *Alp* is a Turkish honorific meaning 'brave' or 'hero'.

perfect and the last opportunity for the Hindu kings, the Kabul *Shahis*, to recover their territories usurped by the cow-eating *Mlecchas*. They formed an alliance with Abu Ali Lawik, the last ruler of Zabul, and began the recovery efforts led by the indomitable warrior Jayapala, the king of Udbhandapur, who was in no mood to let go of Kabul so easily. He assembled a massive confederacy of troops from such diverse regions as Delhi, Ajmer, Kalinjara and Kanauj and attacked Sabuktigin in 986–987. The pitched battle lasted several days, and casualties were high on both sides. Then, the weather played spoilsport, and Jayapala was forced to negotiate for peace. However, it wasn't an offer of surrender. In the letter to Sabuktigin, he thundered:

> You know the nobleness of Hindus. They fear not death or destruction. In affairs of honour and fame we would place ourselves upon the fire like roast meat, and upon the dagger like the sunrays.[74]

And to reinforce this, he sent ambassadors with variations of the same message:

> You know the customs of the Indian soldiers, particularly the Rajputs, who, if driven to desperation, murder their wives and children, set fire to their houses and property, let loose their hair, and rushing on the enemy, are heedless of death, in order to obtain revenge.[75]

Sabuktigin acceded to the peace offer, which was short-lived. Eventually, hostilities resumed, and Jayapala and his

---

[74] Misra, *Indian Resistance to Muslim Invaders up to 1206 A.D.*, 33.
[75] Col John Briggs, *History of the Rise of the Mahomedan Power in India till the Year A.D. 1612*, Vol. 1, trans. from Firishta's *Tarikh-i Firishta* (Calcutta: Cambray & Co, 1908), 17.

Hindu army was defeated and driven out of Kabul. Jayapala was perhaps the last Hindu ruler to show this indefatigable spirit of aggression, appearing as he did at the close of that fateful century—as we shall see.

With Jayapala out of the way, Sabuktigin launched a conquering spree and pocketed Balkh[76] in the north, Helmand in the west and the Indus River region of modern Pakistan. His moment of triumph arrived when the Caliph recognised his governorship of Ghazni.

Elsewhere in mainland India, in 974, the Rashtrakuta Empire had sputtered to death at the hands of its feudatory, the Chalukya king Taila II (or Tailapa II). In its wake, a long and bitter war broke out between Taila II and Paramara Munja, the ruler of Malwa. Munja was ultimately captured and killed sometime between 995 and 997. Taila II lived for barely a year after that.

In the same year, Sabuktigin died, and Abu-l-Qasim Mahmud, his elder son, revolted against his younger brother Ismail who had been appointed as Sabuktigin's successor. After a long-drawn battle[77], Mahmud broke open Ismail's ranks, captured him and threw him in prison in 998. And then, Mahmud of Ghazni turned his attention to India.

Ancient India vanished forever. Medieval Muslim India began.

---

[76] Northern Afghanistan, about 75 km from the Uzbekistan border. It was the capital of Bactria.
[77] Battle of Ghazni.

CHAPTER 2

The Turushka Barbarian Barges into the Living Room

Notwithstanding the successes of Mahmud of Ghazni, India remained practically independent until its absorption into the Empire during the reign of Akbar
H.M. Elliot and John Dowson

If ancient India vanished forever with the invasion of Mahmud of Ghazni, the sputtering vestiges of the Arab Muslims in India also disappeared around the same time. From this point onwards, large parts of India would witness and suffer the prolonged, ruthless and oppressive domination of Turkish Muslim rule for more than four hundred years. To the native Indian tongue, the word 'Turushka' evoked repellent connotations of barbarism, Hindu genocide, forcible conversions, wholesale gangrape of their women, repeated and large-scale temple destructions, mindless cow slaughter and industrial-scale slave-taking. Like the Arab Muslims, the Turushkas were *Mlecchas* as well but they were a particularly abominable subset.

The Turkish domination was built on the smoking embers of the Abbasid Caliphate and the Tahirid and Samanid dynasties. In the 990s, two Turkish families divided the remnants of the Samanid empire between themselves. The Ilak Khans of Turkistan captured Bukhara and by 999, finished off whatever remained of the Samanids, gaining absolute control of all territories to the north of Oxus[1]. The territories lying to the south were swallowed by the Yaminis, popularly known to Indians as the Ghaznavids. The founder of the Ghaznavid dynasty, as we have seen, was Sabuktigin, a fifteen-year-old boy-slave purchased by Alp-Tigin in the thriving slave market[2] at Bukhara. Alp-Tigin was so infatuated with this handsome young teenager that he eventually promoted him to the status of a general, which in due course led to the founding of the Ghaznavid Empire. His son Mahmud was its most bigoted and barbaric but gifted military leader and diabolical warlord. And in 1000, when he turned his attention to mainland India, he intuitively recognised that it was vulnerable as never before and decided to exploit it to the fullest extent.

This is the India he saw.

The Hindu kingdoms in mainland India were euphorically unaware of Mahmud's religion-fuelled imperial vision of a savage, total war of conquest from the vantage of the citadel in Ghazni. By then, centuries of civilisational amnesia had crept into their consciousness. Hindu kings had largely forgotten what K.M. Munshi calls the 'Aryavarta Consciousness' which 'threw up values and institutions of great vigour and tenacity'[3] and for centuries, had enabled them to easily ward off and drive away alien invasions from the time of Alexander, the Bactrian Greeks, the Kushanas, the Sakas and the Huns. It was the same Aryavarta Consciousness that had produced the ascetic

---

[1] Amu Darya.
[2] For a fuller discussion, see C. Scott Levi, 'Hindus beyond the Hindu Kush: Indians in the Central Asian Slave Trade', *Journal of the Royal Asiatic Society*, 12(3) (2002): 277–288.
[3] Munshi, "Foreword," *The History and Culture of the Indian People*, Vol. 5, viii.

Chanakya Kautilya, one of the world's greatest political philosophers, economists and statesman-strategists. This Consciousness had endowed India with a continuous vigour and vitality, which was precisely what enabled them to swat away the repeated Arab incursions in Sindh for *three centuries*. As we've seen in the previous chapter, by the mid- and late 10th century, these Hindu kingdoms had recklessly squandered all of this millennia-old civilisational vigour through unwise, unnecessary infighting. All that they now possessed were the mere outward trappings and not the *spirit* embodied in the Vedas that

> Aryavarata was the sacred land of Dharma, the elevated path to Heaven and to Moksha; where men were nobler than the Devatas themselves; where all knowledge, thought and worship were rooted in the Vedas, revealed by the Devatas themselves.[4]

Even worse, these Hindu kingdoms naively, literally and *foolishly* took for granted, for example, Medhatithi's dictum that

> Aryavarta was so called because the Aryas sprang up in it again and again. Even if it was overrun by the mlechchhas, they could never abide there for long.[5]

Apart from Medhatithi, there was also the widespread belief among Hindu rulers and the general populace that 'whenever a crisis arose, a *Chakravartin*, a world-emperor, would rise in the land and re-establish Dharma.'[6] In the

---

[4] *Vishnupuranam*, II, 3, 4; trans. and paraphrased by the author.
[5] See Medhatithi's commentary on *Manusmriti* in Ganganath Jha, *Manusmriti with the Manubhasya of Medhatithi* (Calcutta: University of Calcutta, 1926), II.22.
[6] Munshi, "Foreword," *The History and Culture of the Indian People*, Vol. 5, x.

10th century, this belief was a precursor to the pervasive fatalism that eventually afflicted the Hindu psyche across large parts of an India under a five-century Muslim domination, as we shall see. However, this belief in the assured, future rise of a Chakravartin had a solid basis in the reality of Bharatavarsha's history so far, where the ancient Dharma had repeatedly triumphed (the repulsions of Greeks and Huns, among several others). This was for a fundamental reason, which is again rooted in the Vedic genius: the victory of Dharma was guided, complemented, safeguarded and sustained... and sustained by Kshatra, or the spirit of valour. One of the core elements or qualities of the spirit of Kshatra[7] is to maintain equilibrium at all levels: individual, social and political. The quality of civilisational stability and sustenance is also built into this spirit of Kshatra. Or, in a more contemporary idiom,

> In the history of the world, it is only Hinduism that gave not only to India but to all her neighbours an organic conception of society based upon economic as well as spiritual needs ... it attempted to mitigate the evil consequences of great disparity by aiming at only the essentials.... *Liberty and law were synthesized to achieve spiritual freedom* [emphasis added].[8]

With the downfall of the Gupta Empire, this integrated and holistic vision of Indian civilisation was lost forever[9], and the successive Hindu empires that emerged upon its

---

[7] For a detailed and in-depth discussion on Kshatra from the Vedic era up to the modern times, see the English translation of Shatavadhani Dr R. Ganesh's Kannada text *Bharatiya Kshatra Parampare* in R. Ganesh, 'The Tradition of Kshatra in India', *Prekshaa Journal*, last accessed 19 August 2019, https://www.prekshaa.in/series-list/The%20Tradition%20of%20Kshaatra%20in%20India.

[8] Dr S. Srikanta Sastri, *Geopolitcs of India and Greater India* (Bangalore: Madhu Publishers, 1943).

[9] Munshi, "Foreword," *The History and Culture of the Indian People*, Vol. 3, x.

wreckage were uniformly, consistently one-eyed. The Hindu kingdoms on the anvil of the barbaric raid of Mahmud of Ghazni were not lacking in Kshatra. What they had lost was the *integral* spirit of Kshatra so indispensable for sustaining their ancient Dharma. K.M. Munshi echoes this tragic spiritual loss of civilisation in the following words:

> The consciousness in [the] political aspect [of the Aryavarta consciousness] had all but disappeared during the few decades which preceded A.D. 1000 on account of the recurring upheavals in North India. The empire of Kanauj, which had stabilised North India for well-nigh 150 years and supported the Shahi kings of the North-West, had disintegrated. Now *Raghukulabhuchakravarti*, 'the World-Emperor of Raghu's race', *was merely a symbol of a vanished greatness* [emphasis added], ruling over a small territory around Kanauj on the sufferance of his erstwhile feudatories.[10]

But there was something even worse that the Hindu kings were endowed with: the aforementioned code of war ethics. If belief in a future liberating Chakravartin was in the realm of hope, this Hindu code of war ethics realistically belonged in the realm of sheer physical survival especially when faced with an unscrupulous invader like Mahmud of Ghazni. As history shows, these Hindu kings went to war armed with the following sacrosanct weapons: no matter how grave the enemy's provocation, the temple, the *murti*, the shrine, the cow and the *Brahmana* were not to be touched. War was a privilege accorded only to the Kshatriyas (or those who enrolled for a life of military honour), and harming the civilian population was a serious lapse of the Kshatriya Dharma. The chastity of women, which was held in divine

---

[10] Munshi, "Foreword," *The History and Culture of the Indian People*, Vol. 5, x.

reverence[11] by the Kshatriya warriors, was inviolable. When we survey this aspect of history, we also find that the Hindu kings on the threshold of Mahmud of Ghazni's invasion had apparently learnt no lessons from the bestial appetizer of an alien Muslim raid that Muhammad bin Qasim had served about three centuries ago.

'I vow to undertake a holy war against Hind every year!'

When Mahmud surveyed this scene from his palace in the city of Ghazni, the Jewel, the capital of the Ghaznavid Empire, he smiled at the prospect of the assured victories and the splendid wealth that was ripe for his picking. As far as he was concerned, he was a staunch practitioner of the Islamic tradition of war in which there was no honour, only victory—absolute and total. Like his father Sabuktigin, the sword of Mahmud 'had a double sanctification'[12] as he set out to maraud India. The campaign was to be brandished in service of the battle of the Only True Faith 'under the crescent and green banner of Islam against the infidels and idolaters of Hindustan', whereupon a 'rich reward of booty' lay in wait for this doughty commander of Islam. That there could be such a thing as a code of war ethics didn't exist even in the realm of hypothesis for another reason. Mahmud was accustomed to the kind of wars fought in Central Asia where it was only about 'the destruction of the enemies and … appropriating their womenfolk. No code circumscribed the destructive zeal of the conqueror; no canon restrained the ruthlessness of their hordes.'[13]

---

[11] Devi-Swaroopa, akin to a Mother Goddess.
[12] A.V. Williams Jackson (ed.), *History of India*, Vol. 5 (New York: Columbia University Press, 1906), 34.
[13] Munshi, "Foreword," *The History and Culture of the Indian People*, Vol. 5, xii.

Besides, Mahmud had discovered an important secret in his battle against Jayapala: that the use of filthy and vile tactics against Hindus on battlefield yields rich harvest—for example, the use of faeces[14] mixed in water and splashed liberally on the fighting Hindu warriors.

But before he seriously cast his eyes in the direction of mainland India, Mahmud spent about two years completing an unfinished business. With a few deft moves, he was able to exert complete sway over the entire northwestern region of Afghanistan by annexing Herat, Bamiyan and Balkh. In 999, he extinguished the last of the Samanid kings, Abdul Malik, and occupied Khorasan. An overjoyed Caliph al-Qadir Billah sent a royal robe of investment to Mahmud and showered the titles of 'Yamin-ud-Daulah'[15] and 'Amin-ul-Millah'[16]. Thus was born the first sultan of Ghazni. This is how Abu Nasr Muhammad Utbi, the secretary and chronicler of Mahmud of Ghazni describes the grand event:

> The sultan sat on his throne and vested himself with his new Khila't, the robe, professing his allegiance to the successor of the prophet of God. The Amirs of Khorasan stood before him in order, with respectful demeanour, and did not take their seats till so directed. He then bestowed upon the nobles, his slaves, his confidential servants, and his chief friends valuable robes and choice presents, beyond all calculation, and *vowed that every year he would undertake a holy war against Hind* [emphasis added].[17]

---

[14] Briggs, *History of the Rise of the Mahomedan Power in India till the Year A.D. 1612*, Vol. 1, 16.
[15] Literally, the 'Right Hand of the Caliphate'.
[16] Literally, the 'Keeper or Protector of the Nation of Islam'.
[17] Abu Nasr Muhammad Utbi, "Kitab-i-Yamini," in *The History of India*, Vol. 5, ed. A. V. Williams Jackson (New York: Columbia University Press, 1906), 42.

The preface at Peshawar

Peshawar was the first city that Mahmud selected for the maiden expedition of his holy war against Hind in 1001. This ancient city originally named Purushapura (City of Men), invaluable in the geostrategic realm as the gateway to the historic Khyber Pass, would get a taste of renewed savagery that paled in comparison to its long-forgotten destruction at the hands of the Huns. Purushapura was perhaps the most pre-eminent city of the Gandhara region and retained its fame for nearly half a millennium. The general region was Vaēkərəta, or Gandhara, the sixth (or seventh) most beautiful city on earth created by Ahura Mazda[18] himself. It was the crown jewel of Bactria and held sway over Takshashila, perhaps the greatest university town of the ancient world. During the pre-Mauryan period, it was the western capital of the Gandhara Mahajanapada. After Alexander's death, his successor, Seleucus Nicator, ceded it to Chandragupta Maurya who further enhanced its prestige. It later became the capital of the Kushan Empire with its magnificent Buddhist stupa built by Kanishka. At its zenith, the vibrant Purushapura was an awesome cultural amalgam pulsating with excellence in art, sculpture, architecture and philosophy. Archaeological excavations and extant coinage of the period reveal a picture[19] of an extraordinary cultural and artistic fusion of Hindu, Buddhist and Hellenistic schools. Purushapura was also perhaps the most important centre of the Gandhara School of Art.

Mahmud of Ghazni selected Peshawar for a fundamental reason: his old harasser, the gritty Jayapala, was still around

---

[18] Zend Avesta: Zarathustra
[19] See, for example, "Gandhara Art," in *Enclycopaedia Britannica*, online edition, https://www.britannica.com/art/Gandhara-art and Ananda K. Coomaraswamy, *The Origin of the Buddha Image* (New Delhi: Munshiram Manoharlal Publishers, 2001).

and in no mood to submit. Quite the contrary. He was determined to wipe out the alien *Mlecchas* from the region for good. The battle theatre was a mixed bag of ambition, retribution, fanaticism, destiny and short-sightedness.

Mahmud's newly robed prestige and authority bestowed by the Caliphate's recognition enabled him to command arms and armies at will. His vassals and subordinates and chieftains agreed to furnish one lakh men whenever he wished. Then he convened a war council in which he declared that he sought Allah's blessings to 'raise the standard of Islam', of widening its dominions in Hind and to bring the full light and the strength of justice of the Only True Faith in this land of darkness and injustice. Writing in hindsight, the historian Utbi is certainly convinced that Mahmud was indeed guided by the light of Allah who also bestowed dignity on him and gave him superb victories in Hind.

Mahmud pitched his tent outside the city that was home to Jayapala, 'the enemy of God'. However, Jayapala had already been proactive, unlike Dahir. This 'villainous infidel' launched the offensive with a solid troop strength comprising twelve thousand horsemen, thirty thousand foot soldiers and three hundred elephants, which met Mahmud's fifteen-thousand-strong cavalry and a few hundred foot soldiers. However, the weather played spoilsport, 'amid the blackness of clouds'. Besides, Jayapala had had previous experience of battle with these *Mlecchas*—with a much-younger Mahmud who had served as a general under Sabuktigin. He used the strategy of calculated withdrawal to buy time, to wait for more reinforcements and avoided direct conflict for days. However, banking on a shrewd and daring gamble, Mahmud attacked Jayapala first, taking him by surprise. Confusion was the first response from Jayapala's unprepared army, led by the elephant force which formed its mainstay. His soldiers, suddenly jolted by this unexpected assault, began shooting arrows wildly and randomly, killing and wounding fellow soldiers. The military defence quickly turned into a chaotic melee. Disorder replaced discipline. The battle lasted just a few hours, at the end of which Utbi gloats how

> the Mussulmans defeated their obstinate opponents, and quickly put them to a complete rout. Noon had not arrived when they had wreaked their vengeance on the enemies of God, killing fifteen thousand of them, spreading them like a carpet over the ground, and making them food for beasts and birds of prey.[20]

Characteristically, Utbi attributes Mahmud's victory to the ignorance of the infidels about the word of the Only True God. He quotes the Quran in support of his claim: Oftentimes a small army overcomes a large one by the order of God.[21]

Like Muhammed bin Qasim, but only with greater savagery, Mahmud of Ghazni gave 'the enemy of God', Jayapala, the first-hand experience of being a prisoner of an Islamic war. His children, grandchildren, relatives, nephews, generals and the 'chief men of his tribe' were bound with ropes and 'carried before the Sultan, like as evildoers, *on whose faces the fumes of infidelity are evident, who are covered with the vapours of misfortune, will be bound and carried to Hell* [emphasis added]'.[22]

And like Qasim, Mahmud next plundered Jayapala's dominion, stripping everyone, including non-combatant

---
[20] Abu Nasr Muhammad Utbi, "Tarikh Yamini," in H.M. Elliot and John Dowson, *The History of India as Told by Its Own Historians*, Vol. 2 (London: Trubner & Co, 1869), 25–7.
[21] Quran 2:249
[22] Utbi, "Tarikh Yamini," 26.

citizens, of pearls, shining gems, rubies and gold. The additional booty included the thousands of slaves, 'beautiful men and women'. Returning to his camp, Mahmud said a prayer of thanks to 'Allah, the lord of the universe'. Utbi gives the date of this 'splendid and celebrated action' as 27 November 1001.

But an even worse fate awaited Jayapala.

As an Asuravijayi, this is what Mahmud did, in the glowing words of Utbi:

> The Sultan directed that the polluted infidel Jaipal should be paraded about, so that his sons and chieftains might see him in that condition of shame, bonds, and disgrace and that the fear of Islam might fly abroad through the country of the infidels.[23]

Mahmud of Ghazni then freed Jayapala on the condition of receiving fifty elephants plus two lakh dirhams, till which time he had to leave his son and grandson as hostages. This is perhaps the first in an uncountable line of such hostage-taking of Hindu princes, an act which the British reciprocated in the last years of the 18th century, by taking Tipu Sultan's young sons as postwar hostages till he paid up war damages.

Jayapala's end was truly befitting his life as an unsullied warrior: fearless, courageous, proud, uncompromising and honourable. He wrote to his son and declared to his citizens that he was unfit to rule any longer. He had let them down, and he himself had been degraded. Death was preferable to a life of shame and dishonour. Towards the end of 1001, this noble Kshatriya, according to the code of his ancient Dharma so dear to him, to preserve which he fought continuously, shaved off his head, lay down on a pyre and set fire to it—and to himself.

---

[23] Ibid., 26–7.

However, as far as Mahmud was concerned, Peshawar was only the preface of a decade-plus tale of inveterate brutality that he would unleash on mainland India. The years 1002 and 1003 kept him busy in quelling troubles in Sistan (Sijistan).

'The fire which Allah has lighted for infidels'

In 1004, Mahmud began to write the first chapter of the aforementioned dark story. With a sizeable army comprising the most competent route guides and standard bearers, he marched through Sibi,[24] crossed the Sindhu River near Multan and reached the solidly fortified city of Bhatiya.[25] As he surveyed it, Mahmud admired the manner in which the massive fort radiated an aura of impregnability. Even 'the wings of an eagle could not surmount' its forbidding walls. The moat that surrounded it was as wide and deep as an ocean. As with every Hindu-ruled town and city of varying sizes, Bhatiya was extremely prosperous and as wealthy as 'imagination could conceive in terms of property, armies and military weapons'. Bhatiya was ruled by Baji Rai[26], a vassal of Anandapala, son of the extraordinary martyr, Jayapala. Like Raja Dahir and Jayapala in his final battle, Baji Rai committed a cardinal error of strategy. Indeed, it appears that barring almost a handful of instances, Hindu kings and generals and commanders repeatedly and foolishly sacrificed strategy at the altar of false bravado and perhaps overconfidence in superior numbers or military might. Instead of outwaiting or wearing out Mahmud, he charged *out of his fort*, relying mostly on the infallibility of his elephant force, and met the enemy. The

---
[24] In Baluchistan.
[25] The exact name of the city is still a matter of historical debate. See Majumdar, *The History and Culture of the Indian People*, Vol. 5, 7.
[26] The exact profile and antecedents of Baji Rai are unclear. Utbi calls him Biji Rai while Firishta calls him Baji Rai, the vassal of Anandapala.

first three of the four-day-long battle witnessed substantial casualties on the Muslim side, which stared at defeat. On the fourth day, Mahmud decided to take the ultimate gamble and was rewarded. He correctly targeted the elephant force that formed the centre and the main strength of Baji Rai's formation and shattered it. By evening, Baji Rai retreated to the fort. But Mahmud was unrelenting. He stormed the city gates, occupied it, filled up the moat, hacked at the narrow roads, opened up the closed entrances and further widened other key entrances of the city, making it impossible for Baji Rai to defend. Baji Rai ultimately fled from the fort, crossed the Sindhu, disappeared in the darkness of the thick jungle and hid in a hill nearby. However, Mahmud's contingent which had pursued him, eventually located and surrounded his meagre force. Unwilling to be taken prisoner, Baji Rai took out his dagger and thrust it into his heart. Utbi characterises Baji Rai's final fate as going to 'the fire which Allah has lighted for infidels'.

Meanwhile, Mahmud and his men hungrily gorged on Bhatiya, pillaging the city and slaughtering the idolaters at will. As the Islam-ordained share of war spoils, Mahmud kept one hundred and twenty of the two hundred and eighty elephants and a proportionate amount of precious metals and war arsenal. Bhatiya was now under the sword of Islam. However, there was still some unfinished business. As a pious Ghazi and Protector of the Only True Faith, Mahmud sent for a bunch of Orthodox Islamic clergy and converted the surviving Hindus to Islam en masse. Utbi describes the event in pious language.

> Mahmud remained at Bhatia till he had cleansed it from pollution, and appointed a person there to teach those who had embraced Islam, and lead them in the right way.[27]

---

[27] Utbi, "Tarikh Yamini," 30.

Triumphant and overjoyed, Mahmud thanked God and left for Ghazni in 1005 with his newly acquired, substantial booty when the full fury of the monsoon was lashing the region. The generous rivers that continued to bestow such perennial bounty upon Punjab without asking were now transformed into amorphous, surging liquid monsters that swallowed almost all of Mahmud's haul and gobbled his men as they tried to cross the waters. However, what little booty Mahmud took back to Ghazni was still substantial.

'The conquest of India is the conquest of culture by those who lacked it'

By the time Mahmud's career of the jihadi conquest of India was beginning to take concrete shape, Multan had irreversibly lapsed into an Islamic outpost. In the interim following Muhammd bin Qasim's exit, the city was ruled by a long line of unmemorable chieftains.

But by the early to mid-10th century, the savage 'revolution' unleashed by the Qarmatians[28] against the tottering Abbasid Caliphate spread its ripples to the frontiers of India as well. They impelled a 'century of terror', catapulting the Ismaili Shia political power to an unprecedented—and unrepeatable—zenith under the semi-barbaric ruler, Abu Sa'id al-Jannabi. The Qarmatians declared that the Hajj pilgrimage to Mecca was a superstition and instigated an endless series of brutal raids against pilgrims crossing the Arabian peninsula. In one instance, they slaughtered a whopping twenty thousand in one go. The most audacious climax to this deluge of brutal annihilation was reached in 930 when al-Jannabi's marauding forces sacked *both* Mecca

---

[28] Also transliterated as 'Carmathian', 'Qarmathian' or 'Karmathian'.

and Medina. Mecca was the special target[29] of the inveterate Qarmatian hatred towards the Sunnis. They filled the holy Zamzam Well within Mecca itself with heaps of corpses of the Hajj pilgrims they had butchered indiscriminately. To add further insult to injury, they carted off the Black Stone at Kaaba from Mecca to al-Ahsa (Eastern Arabia) and forced the Abbasids to pay a massive ransom for its return. It was the ultimate humiliation. The entire Muslim world was outraged but helpless because the final authority, the Caliph himself cowered in fear before the Qarmatian wrath. For the first time since Islam became a military religion to reckon with, the annual Hajj pilgrimage—the fifth pillar of Islam—was halted for *eight* years, a measure of the level of the mortal terror that the Qarmatians had instilled in the psyche of the Muslim world.

Elsewhere, a branch of these ascendant and all-powerful Qarmatians had managed to gain control of Multan, and in the early 10th century, it was ruled by a minor chieftain named Abu'l-Fath Da'ud. Shrewdly realising his own limitations, Da'ud had, early on, entered into a friendly alliance with Sabuktigin. He continued this alliance with Mahmud as well. However, with Mahmud, this relationship was uneasy and wholly unequal: Da'ud feared Mahmud while Mahmud merely tolerated Da'ud, a heretic but a Muslim still. This uneasy relationship reached its breaking point when Mahmud received intelligence that Da'ud continued to commit the unpardonable crime of evangelising and spreading his heretical Ismaili sect, which injected 'impurity in his religion' and 'seditious designs in his heart'. To Sultan Mahmud, the pious Sunni Muslim, this act was a punishable

---

[29] See "Mecca," in *Encyclopaedia Britannica*, online edition, https://www.britannica.com/place/Mecca; "Carmatians," in *Encyclopaedia Iranica*, online edition, http://www.iranicaonline.org/articles/carmatians-ismailis (for a detailed list of primary sources).

offence. By death. It was equivalent to that other crime in Islam: *irtidad* or apostasy. And so, the sultan, 'zealous for the Mohammedan religion, thought it a shame to allow him to retain his government while he practiced such wickedness and disobedience, and he besought the assistance of the gracious God in bringing him to repentance'.[30]

But before Mahmud could punish Da'ud, he had to encounter opposition in Anandapala, the son and successor of Jayapala. Anandapala had allied with and offered protection to Da'ud against Mahmud. Needless to say, it was a tactical alliance. Anandapala was constantly on the wait to avenge Jayapala's death and lived his life in the hope of wresting his lost territories and driving Mahmud even out of Ghazni. Utbi recounts what happened next.

> The sultan ... [attacked] Rai [Anandapala] first ... to bow down his broad neck, to cut down the trees of his jungles, to destroy everything he possessed, and thus to obtain the fruit of two paradises by this double conquest. He accordingly stretched out ... the hand of slaughter, imprisonment, pillage, depopulation, and fire, and hunted him ... until ... he fled ... to ... Kashmir.[31]

Yet another flame of Hindu resistance in this region was extinguished, partly due to Anandapala's misplaced generosity of putting his neck on the line for Da'ud, another theme that recurs throughout the prolonged history of Hindu defence against Muslim invasions.

When he heard of Anandapala's fate, a mortally scared Da'ud abandoned Multan and fled to a nondescript island on the Sindhu River. However, the heavily garrisoned

---

[30] Utbi, "Tarikh Yamini", 30. See also, Munshi, "Foreword," *The History and Culture of the Indian People*, Vol. 5, x.
[31] Utbi, "Tarikh Yamini," 31.

Multan did not yield easily. After a siege of seven days, Mahmud finally shattered the defences open with brutal assault. The hapless citizens pleaded with him to spare their lives in exchange for twenty lakh dirhams.[32] He accepted. What he did not accept was the proposal to spare the infernal Qarmatians. Mahmud rounded up hundreds of these heretics in Multan, and in a majority of cases, he personally carried out a horrific genocide on a scale and with a savagery that has few parallels. Both Utbi and the *Adab-ul-Muluk wa Kifayat al Mamluk*[33] give graphic accounts of the genocide. The latter work which mentions that Sultan Mahmud slaughtered so many Qarmatians, states that

> a stream of blood flowed from the Lohari gate which was on the western side of the town ... and ... the hand of the Sultan was stuck fast to the hilt of the sword on account of congealed blood, and had to be immersed in a bath of hot water before it could be loosened.[34]

Next, Mahmud thoroughly desecrated the Ismaili mosque and 'reduced it to the humble position of a barn-floor' where henna leaves were stitched.

The news and fame of Mahmud of Ghazni's exploits in Sindh spread like wildfire throughout the Muslim world, 'over distant countries, and over the salt sea[35], even as far as Egypt'. Utbi further gloats how

---

[32] According to some scholars, this amount is vastly exaggerated, but at any rate, the sum must have been substantial to evoke the feeling of mercy in Mahmud.
[33] Meaning, Rules for the Kings and the Welfare of the Subjects.
[34] Muhammad Nazim, *The Life and Times of Sultan Mahmud of Ghazna* (Cambridge: Cambridge University Press, 1931), 97.
[35] Arabian Sea.

Sind and her sister (Hind) trembled at his power and vengeance his celebrity exceeded that of Alexander the Great, and heresy (ilhad), rebellion, and enmity, were suppressed.[36]

However, an overlooked underlying historical fact is that both Sabuktigin and his son Mahmud had to wage wars unabated for fifteen long years to finally wipe out the Hindu Shahi kings in the region of Afghanistan and modern Pakistan. Al-Biruni's testimony provides first-hand evidence of this fact in a glowing tribute that he pays them.

> The Hindu Shahiya dynasty is now extinct, and of the whole house, there is no longer the slightest remnant in existence. *We must say that, in all their grandeur, they never slackened in the ardent desire of doing that which is good and right, that they were men of noble sentiment and noble bearing* [emphasis added].[37]

K.M. Munshi's pithy comment on this sorry end of the Hindu Shahi kings is simultaneously blunt and evocative: '*The conquest of India is the conquest of culture by those who lacked it* [emphasis added].'[38]

The barbarian barges into the living room

It is beyond the scope of this work to give a full and comprehensive account of *all* the barbaric incursions that Mahmud of Ghazni made in mainland India. In the overall assessment, it suffices to mention that for the first time, it

---

[36] Utbi, "Tarikh Yamini," 32.
[37] Edward C. Sachau, *Alberuni's India*, Vol. 2 (London: Kegan Paul, Trench, Trubner & Co, 1910), 13.
[38] K.M. Munshi, *Somanatha: The Shrine Eternal* (Bombay: Bharatiya Vidya Bhavan, 1965), 32.

was Mahmud who audaciously smashed the defences of mainland India in an unprecedented fashion and 'shook the very foundations of life in India as her people had known it until then'. The macabre forces that he unleashed gave birth to what Munshi and other scholars call the Age of Resistance, which lasted till the late 18th century: till the downfall of Aurangzeb and to a lesser extent, Tipu Sultan. Beginning with 1004 up to his last raid in 1027, there was almost no region north of the Vindhya mountains that Mahmud did not ravage and plunder. The kind of all-out warfare that had so far been restricted only to a few pockets of Sindh and Afghanistan was now introduced in all these regions. Hindus were suddenly rudely jolted awake to a wholly unfamiliar, living nightmare when Mahmud's armies overwhelmed the sacred Indo-Gangetic plain, the nucleus of their ancient *punyabhoomi,* the hordes of his locust-like barbarians setting fire to its fertile, green, smiling plains, plundering, indulging in indiscriminate massacre of innocent citizens, gangraping women, enslaving boys, girls, men, women and children, destroying ancient cities and centres of learning, art and culture, razing magnificent temples sanctified by uninterrupted centuries of nationwide devotion, smashing *murtis* and enforcing an alien religion at the point of the sword and fire.

The barbarian at the gate had barged right into the living room and had enslaved the house owner.

A chief factor that enabled Mahmud of Ghazni to wreak such extensive havoc across such a vast expanse of India lies in his eventual conquest of (undivided) Punjab, the original region of the sacred Pancha-Nada Kshetra (land of the five rivers), which was the highway to mainland India. With this single masterstroke, he opened up mainland India to the ravenous plunderers from Central Asia who eagerly enlisted in Mahmud's force as freelance mercenaries. Thus, 'thousands of trans-frontier Turks and Pathans flocked to the conquering sultan's banner every autumn.'[39] They were not looking for employment or salary but only permission to plunder whatever they could in his terrain. The deed accomplished, they would return to their abodes in the treacherous and freezing mountains of Central Asia until the next bout of ravaging. This is remarkably similar to the freelance, loot-hungry marauders from Damascus who had joined Muhammad bin Qasim's army about three centuries ago—it holds an important lesson of history.

In less than twenty years, Mahmud reduced Thaneshwar, Mathura, Kanauj, and Prabhas Patan[40] to smouldering wreckages. That's an enormous sweep of the country encompassing modern Haryana, Uttar Pradesh and Gujarat. However, the serial destructive raids of Mahmud were not entirely unchecked. The proud Kshatriya king Vidyadhara Chandela, ruling from the Jejakabhukti region[41], halted Mahmud's victorious march in the east at Kalinjara[42]. The next was the mighty Paramaradeva Bhoja, one of the greatest military commanders, emperors and multifaceted scholars the world has known. Mahmud had already heard about the fearsome reputation of Bhoja and wisely chose to keep his distance.

Then he turned his eyes in the direction of the fabled Somanatha Temple in faraway Gujarat and eventually accomplished a feat that would immortalise his infamy, or religious piety, depending on one's yardstick of humanity. Mahmud was propelled by a more fundamental reason to conquer Somanatha. By 1023, he increasingly began to hear a constant refrain emerging from various quarters of

---

[39] Sarkar, *Military History of India*, 24.
[40] Prabhasa Pattana, home to the grand Somanatha Temple.
[41] Modern-day Bundelkhand.
[42] Modern-day Kalinjar near Khajuraho.

the infidels: they boasted that Mahmud could break all those thousands of idols and temples in northern India only because all these sites no longer enjoyed the protection of the mighty Somanatha. Then the infidels went one step further and *dared* the sultan to touch Somanatha. That challenge decided the matter. Mahmud made a vow that by destroying this accursed idol temple, he would chop off the very roots of this dark faith of idolatry.

But-shikhan not *but-farosh!*

Monday. 18 October 1025.

Mahmud of Ghazni knelt on the ground in prayer and asked the blessing of Allah 'upon his arms'. Then he set out of his capital Ghazni, leading a massive army that included thirty thousand regular cavalry. Only the best would do for this dangerous adventure. His support cortège also comprised thirty thousand camels that carried water and provisions. Apart from this, each trooper had his own mini-retinue of two camels to supply water. About three weeks later, Mahmud reached Multan, rested there for a while and on 26 November, began his expedition proper. His earlier experience of an unfruitful siege at Kalinjara had taught him a lesson he didn't forget: the main portion of the Ganga–Jamuna belt was still fully under the control of powerful infidel kings and was, therefore, an unsafe route to take. And so, from Multan, Mahmud marched downwards towards the deadly Thar desert, which was 'fiery as Jahannum itself'. It was sheer recklessness motivated by nothing but naked ambition and goaded by a kind of indomitable inner jubilation of a foregone victory: of acquiring loot that would surpass everything he had acquired so far. The scorching Thar was overpowered by Mahmud's inflamed grit.

Meanwhile at Anahilapataka[43], Bhima, the current ruler of the distinguished Gujarat Chalukya dynasty founded by Mularaja, was fast asleep at the wheel. Somanatha was the guardian deity of Mularaja.

When he emerged from the blazing desert after a gruelling journey, Mahmud stormed the Ludrava town[44] near Jaisalmer and completely wasted it, slaughtering the citadel manned by a small body of soldiers who fought till the last breath but didn't flee. Next, he took the Chikudar hill[45], which was so high that the stars passed[46] below it. Then it was the turn of Nahrwala[47], the capital itself. Which was when the thoroughly unprepared and complacent Bhima fled the scene in advance and sought refuge in the fort of Kanthkot. And thus, by December 1025, in an astonishing span of just over two months, Mahmud was camping outside Patan itself. At this point, the strategist in him chose to take some much-deserved rest after the wearisome desert journey and all that fighting. He replenished his provisions and water and marched towards Mundher or Modhera, home of the fabulous Sun Temple that stands even today as a tourist attraction. Here, he encountered solid resistance from the Hindu army, which he eventually crushed. Then he cut straight across the Kathiawar peninsula and arrived at the opulent town of Dewalwara[48], where he had to again face stiff resistance. His

---

[43] Anahilapataka corresponds to the Patan district of modern Gujarat. It is also known as Anahila Pattana or Anhilvada Patan.
[44] Today, it is the Lodrawa village.
[45] It is hard to precisely identify this hill but it is located somewhere on the Rajasthan–Gujarat border.
[46] Paraphrase of a *qasida* authored by the chronicler and poet, Farrukhi, who accompanied Mahmud on the expedition to Somanatha. The *Tarikh-i-Fakhru'd-Din Mubarakshah* says that Mahmud was so happy at this *qasida* that he gifted an elephant-load of gold to Farrukhi.
[47] In Muslim chronicles, Nahrwala is the name given to Anahilapataka or Patan.
[48] Modern-day Dilwara, famous for its Hindu and Jain temples.

superior force easily overcame it by slaughtering soldiers and unarmed citizens alike. He smashed its temples and looted everything worth looting. It was the final leg of his devastating campaign.

Thursday. 6 January 1026.

Mahmud of Ghazni finally stood outside the gates of the magnificent Somanatha and realised that it wouldn't be easy to take it. The city by the seashore was strongly defended by a fortress with lakhs of devout Hindus inside, willing to do anything to save it. However, by the time Mahmud had encamped there, these devout Hindus had been stricken by a belief that was as cocksure as it was fatal. This is how the historian D.C. Ganguly describes the eve before an epic tragedy of their own making.

> *The Hindus, who assembled on the rampart of the fort, wore* [sic] *passing their time in merry-making, fondly believing that Somanatha had drawn the Muslims there only to annihilate them for the sins they had committed in demolishing idols elsewhere. Their morale was high even though their leader had fled away in cowardice with his family to a neighbouring island* [emphasis added].[49]

Mahmud began his pounding the very next morning. The Hindus hit back with a ferocity and violence that stunned Mahmud and his armies, which quickly retreated for the day. The next day proved even worse for Mahmud. The Hindu defence derived its strength and fury from desperation but it didn't last because it was leaderless against Mahmud's well-organised and superior army. The greater the pushback from the Hindu side, the more determined Mahmud became. As Mahmud's soldiers finally scaled the

---

[49] Majumdar, *The History and Culture of the Indian People*, Vol. 5, 20.

walls of the fort and entered Somanatha, they found the desperate Hindus crowded in front of the gate of the grand Somanatha Temple, which Ganguly describes vividly, in awesome detail.

> The Somanatha Temple stood on huge blocks of stone, and its roof was supported by 56 wooden pillars 'curiously carved and set with precious stones.' The pyramidal roof was made of 13 stories, and was surmounted by fourteen golden domes. The girth of the linga was 4 feet 6 inches, and its height above the base was 7 feet 6 inches. A portion of the linga, 6 feet in height, was hidden beneath the base. Adjacent to it under its pedestal there was the treasury containing many gold and silver miniature idols. The canopy over it was set with jewels and was decorated with rich embroidery. The dark chamber in which the linga was installed was illumined by jewelled chandeliers. In front of the chamber there was a chain of gold, 200 Manns[50] in weight, attached to a bell, which was rung by shaking the chain from time to time for specific purpose. One thousand Brahmanas were appointed to perform the worship of the linga and for conducting the devotees into the temple. There were three hundred barbers for shaving the heads and beards of the pilgrims. Three hundred and fifty persons, both male and female, were employed to sing and dance before the linga every day. All these people received daily allowances from the temple funds. The income of the temple was derived from the 10,000 villages endowed to it, and from the offerings of the devotees. The temple possessed vast wealth in gold, silver, pearls, and rich jewels, which had been accumulated in course of centuries.[51]

---

[50] 1 Mann or Maund = 40 kg.

[51] Ibid. For the most comprehensive account of the Somanatha Temple, see Munshi, *Somanatha: The Shrine Eternal*.

Mahmud of Ghazni annihilated all this painstaking work done over the course of centuries in one brutal sweep of the sword and blaze of the fire. The first step was to slaughter this crowd of panicked, desperate and crestfallen Hindus. The large bands of people who were inside the sprawling temple, praying to their Ishta-Devata Somanatha, the centuries-old, sacred Jyotirlinga, for courage, surged out and charged against Mahmud's soldiers. Batch after batch of such Hindus were pitilessly massacred. The total estimate runs to about fifty thousand. Those who attempted to escape were doggedly hunted down and slaughtered.

It was now time for Sultan Mahmud to crown his savage triumph by stamping it with the twin emblems of the victory of Islam and his credentials as a pious Ghazi. Al-Biruni, Mahmud's chronicler and witness writes:

> The image was destroyed by Prince Mahmud in 416 H. (1026 C.E.). He ordered the upper part to be broken and the remainder to be transported to his residence, Ghaznin, with all its coverings and trappings of gold, jewels and embroidered garments. Part of it has been thrown into the hippodrome of the town, together with the Cakraswamin, an idol of bronze that had been brought from Thaneshar. Another part of the idol from Somnath lies before the door of the mosque of Ghaznin, on which people rub their feet to clean them from dirt and wet.[52]

The later Muslim chronicler Firishta portrays the same vandalism of the Somanatha Temple in this fashion:

> Having now placed guards round the walls and at the gates, Mahmud entered Somnat accompanied by his sons and a few

---

[52] Sachau, *Alberuni's India*, Vol. 2, 103.

of his nobles and principal attendants. On approaching the temple, he saw a superb edifice built of hewn stone.... In the center of the [Temple] hall was Somnat, a stone idol, five yards in height, two of which were sunk in the ground. The King, approaching the image, raised his mace and struck off its nose. *He ordered two pieces of the idol to be broken off and sent to Ghazni so that one might be thrown at the threshold of the public mosque, and the other at the court door of his own palace* [emphasis added]. These identical fragments are to this day (now six hundred years ago) to be seen at Ghazni. Two more fragments were reserved to be sent to Mecca and Medina.... The next blow broke open the belly of Somnat, which was hollow, and discovered a quantity of diamonds, rubies, and pearls.[53]

When a group of distraught Brahmins beseeched Mahmud to halt further destruction of the *murti* in exchange for gold and other wealth, Mahmud was candid:

Should I consent to such a measure, my name would be handed down to posterity as 'Mahmud the idol-seller'[54] whereas I desire to be known as 'Mahmud the idol-destroyer'[55].[56]

After finishing his pervasive plunder, pillage and pogrom of the infidels, Mahmud burned down this sacred temple. Somanatha was now a smoking monument to the wreckage caused by religious piety, a catastrophe which Munshi characterises as follows:

---

[53] Briggs, *History of the Rise of the Mahomedan Power in India till the Year A.D. 1612*, Vol. I, 72.
[54] *but-farosh*.
[55] *but-shikhan*.
[56] Ibid.

> A sacred city like … Somanatha armoured principally by the devotion and reverence of the whole country, fell prey to an army pledged to fanatic destruction of alien shrines.[57]

Tidings of the destruction of Somanatha travelled like wildfire to the corners of the Muslim world. It was celebrated as the crowning glory of Islam over idolatry. Sultan Mahmud overnight became the champion of the Only True Faith. Countless paeans were composed in his honour, as we shall see.

Triumph ends in disaster

But out here, in its immediate aftermath, Mahmud realised the monumental blunder he had committed by destroying Somanatha and smashing the sacred Jyotirlinga itself. He had blazed a daring trail of triumph, striking so deep into this watery corner of mainland India. But he had to return to Ghazni. Safely. With the full weight of the sensational booty he had so cruelly wrested. Encountering the countless infidel kings and chiefs and rulers. These seething warriors would definitely not let him go unpunished. Mahmud received intelligence that they had formed a powerful and united confederacy under the dreaded Paramaradeva Bhoja's leadership with the sole intention of blocking his return, capturing him and slicing off his scalp. He could no longer risk returning to Ghazni via the same route through which he had entered. Paramaradeva Bhoja and the entire Hindu confederacy had not only blocked Kathiawar but began sending their contingents towards him for an offensive. Mahmud had successfully been isolated in Somanatha. And so, he panicked and chose to turn in the direction of Kutch

---

[57] Munshi, *Somanatha: The Shrine Eternal*, 7.

and from there, planned to enter Sindh and reach the safe haven of Multan.

That decision would be the beginning of his troubles.

The first leg of Mahmud's return journey led him to a small inlet of the Arabian Sea between Kathiawar and Kutch. He crossed it with great care—a small misstep would submerge his massive loot. When he emerged on the other side, he saw the great fort of Kanthkot where the panicked Bhima had taken refuge. Now, Bhima fled it as well, when he heard news of Mahmud's approach. Mahmud easily plundered it and added the spoils to his already substantial booty. After days of arduous marching, he reached the borders of Sindh and hired a guide to help him cross the treacherous desert. The guide turned out to be an unlikely hero and avenging angel of sorts. He had successfully concealed his real identity as a great devotee of Somanatha and, under the pretence of helping Mahmud, led his army astray for three days and three nights to a part of the desert where no water could be found for miles. It didn't take long for Mahmud to detect his perfidy and behead him. But considerable damage had already been done by then. The desert had sapped the morale and mind of Mahmud's army and had driven them insane. Firishta narrates how 'many of the troops died raving mad from the intolerable heat and thirst.'[58] The large number of animals that accompanied Mahmud's return perished similarly. Mahmud's dazzling victory was gradually turning into a curse, with disaster riding on its back at every step. After a few more days of this directionless desert wandering, Mahmud finally came to a place where he found water. From there, he somehow managed to reach Mansurah and

---

[58] Briggs, *History of the Rise of the Mahomedan Power in India till the Year A.D. 1612*, Vol. 1, 78.

raided its Qarmatian ruler who immediately scampered away in fright. Eventually, he marched along the upper course of the Sindhu River and reached Multan, not without additional trouble in the form of the proud Jats who were boiling with vengeance. They managed to hack away at a good chunk of the remainder of his tired and dispirited army. Mahmud let them go unpunished for the moment and plodded on, finally reaching Ghazni on 2 April 1026. All that remained with him was a fraction of his formidable army and an even lesser amount of the pillage from his audacious blitzkrieg into Somanatha. It was a truly humiliating and awful end—a splendid victory culminating in ruin.

For the remainder of the four years of his life, Mahmud never ventured into India again.

A backstory of sorts is in order.

The tragic tale of the appalling destruction of the Somanatha Temple had a similarly grand and, therefore, equally barbaric precedent in 1018 at the ancient pilgrimage city of Mathura sanctified by the birth of Sri Krishna.

When Mahmud reached Mathura, what he saw there defied every description he had heard about its splendour. But when he actually beheld the Krishna Temple, even he momentarily surrendered to the involuntary call of its exquisiteness rooted in inexpressible divinity. It was a supreme expression of the primordial human longing for unqualified, stainless spirituality laid out in stone, the cynosure of this ancient centre of Hindu pilgrimage. The impregnable city of Mathura was walled with hard stone, erected upon sturdy and lofty foundations to protect its sanctity from rain, river and ransack. This is what Mahmud wrote when he saw the Krishna Temple:

If anyone should wish to construct a building equal to this, he would not be able to do it without expending a hundred-hundred thousand [i.e., hundred million] red dinars, and it would occupy two hundred years, even though the most experienced and able workmen were employed.[59]

And that's where his momentary admiration stopped. It would be an unpardonable religious travesty to let this magnificent idol temple remain standing. Mahmud ordered his men to douse it with naphtha and set fire to it. Hundreds of other idol temples in Mathura met with the same fate.

The hero of every aspiring Ghazi

Although it ended in disaster, Mahmud's exceptionally bigoted exploits at Somanatha had earned him enormous prestige in the Muslim world. All Muslim chroniclers of Islam's march in India unanimously and glowingly hail Mahmud as one of their greatest conquerors, kings and a champion of the Islamic faith. The Caliph sent him a highly laudatory letter congratulating him on a pious service done to expand the dominions of the Only True Faith, bestowing the grand titles, Right Hand of the Islamic State[60] and Guardian of the Islamic Faith[61]. A scholar of medieval Indian history, Meenakshi Jain accurately captures a core theological reason for the Caliph's glowing praise of Mahmud:

> Mahmud's assault on Somanatha electrified the Muslim world because it was viewed as a sequel to the Prophet's action at Kaba. Muslims identified the Somanatha idol

---

[59] H.M. Elliot and John Dowson, *The History of India as Told by Its Own Historians*, Vol. 2 (London: Trubner & Co, 1869), 44.
[60] Yamin-addaula.
[61] Amin-ul Millat.

as that of Manat[62], believed to have been ferreted out of Mecca just prior to the Prophet's attack on its temple. By destroying Somanatha, therefore, Mahmud was virtually completing the Prophet's work; hence the act was hailed as the crowning glory of Islam over idolatry.[63]

Apart from introducing *Sanatana* Bharatavarsha to the all-out, no-holds-barred, total war of savage conquest and annihilation which included industrial-scale iconoclasm powered by religious fanaticism, Mahmud of Ghazni also initiated that other diabolical precedent: wholesale slave-taking.

From its very inception, slave-taking was an integral element in the Islamic method of warfare, conquest and occupation, a phenomenon pervasive across the Muslim world for centuries. But there is a sharp distinction in the institution of slavery practised by, say, the Egyptians, Greeks

---

[62] Manat was the original and the oldest goddess in pre-Islamic Arabia alongside her sister-goddesses, Al-Lat and Al-'Uzza. She was the goddess of fate, fortune, time, death and destiny and occupied a highly exalted position in the pantheon of pre-Islamic Arabian deities. al-Mushallal, a place between Mecca and Medina, was a famed pilgrimage centre which housed a temple of Manat. She was depicted in wooden portraits and in the form of an idol at the selfsame al-Mushallal. Prophet Muhammad dispatched a force of twenty horsemen under the leadership of Sa'd bin Zaid al-Ashhali to destroy the idol of Manat. Sa'd broke the idol, vandalised the temple and returned victorious. The connection of Manat with Somanatha occurs in the mention of the Ghaznavid court poet, Abul Hasan Ali ibn Julugh Farrukhi Sistani, who says he accompanied Mahmud to Somanatha. He confounds 'Somanath' as 'Su-Manat' and concocts a fanatastic tale that one of the Manat idols in Arabia had been secretly carried all the way here, and Mahmud as the pious Ghazi, broke it as part of the sacred duty he was discharging in service of Islam. For fuller details, refer to: (1) M. J. Akbar, *The Shade of Swords: Jihad and the Conflict Between Islam and Christianity* (New Delhi: Roli Books Private Limited, 2013) (2) William Muir, *The Life of Mahomet and History of Islam, to the Era of the Hegira* (London: Smith, Elder & Co., 1861).

[63] Meenakshi Jain, 'A Review of Romila Thapar's *Somanatha, The Many Voices of a History*', *The Pioneer*, 21 March 2004.

and Romans and by the Islamic world. It was the brilliant military successes in the early years of the rapid expansion of Islam that gets the credit[64] for transforming slave-taking into a flourishing transnational trade that has few parallels in world history. Important slave markets in the Muslim world of that era included Bukhara, Balkh[65], Baghdad, Istanbul, Ghazni and Samarkhand. Prepubescent girls, young women and good-looking boys[66] were especially in great demand. For instance, Sabuktigin was a mere lad of twelve when he was captured as a prisoner of war and sold to a merchant named Nasr, who, after three years, sold him to Alp-Tigin who was besotted with him. Whichever part of India that Mahmud conquered had a vast treasure of such greatly in-demand infidels to be carted off as slaves. More than 90 per cent of these infidels were innocent men, women and children who had played no role in combating the holy war Mahmud had declared against their equally infidel kings. The number of slaves taken by Mahmud is in the order of 'hundreds of thousands'[67]. Every Muslim chronicle, including the *Tarikh-i-Yamini, Tabaqat-i-Akbari, Tarikh-i-Alai* and the *Khulasat-ut-Tawarikh* record the staggering numbers of Hindus Mahmud had taken as slaves. At one point, Utbi records that the slaves had become so lavishly abundant that they had become dirt cheap in these slave markets, and that 'men of respectability in their own native land (India) were degraded by becoming slaves of common shopkeepers

---

[64] A highly recommended book on the subject is Dr K.S. Lal's *Muslim Slave System in Medieval India* (Delhi: Aditya Prakashan, 1994).
[65] The ancient Vahlika or Bahlika or more commonly, Bactria.
[66] For an interesting outline of the different geographical dimensions of slave-taking by medieval Muslim kings, see Majid Sheikh, 'Harking Back: Slaves from Lahore and Punjab', *Dawn*, Karachi, 23 December 2018.
[67] K.S. Lal, "Enslavement of Hindus by Arab and Turkish Invaders" in *Muslim Slave Systems in Medieval India*.

in Ghazni.'[68] The towering scholar and historian, Will Durant echoes Utbi when he says that Mahmud took the infidels back home

> to be sold as slaves; but so great was the number of such captives that after some years no one could be found to offer more than a few shillings for a slave.[69]

Ellenborough rips out the Ghazi's gates

Despite all these apparent successes and the monumental havoc that Mahmud's annual holy war had wreaked in large parts of India, life quickly returned to normal as soon as his threat grew distant and then disappeared. Somanatha, so central to Mahmud's successes in mainland India, presents the most eminent example. In just five years after Mahmud's all-round devastation, the Hindus rebuilt the temple on an even grander scale, and Gujarat became wealthier and more powerful than before. In the same period of reconstruction, the exquisite art at the Dewalwara Temple sprung up from the wounded genius of the *Sanatana* civilisation, a proud artistic and spiritual counterattack against savagery.

But an important footnote to Mahmud's destructive legacy is the fact that he never left behind even a semblance of an empire in mainland India. The Ghaznavid Empire under him stretched only across the expanse of northwestern Iran, Khwarazm and Makran.

However, what he had really left behind were some permanent scars on the Hindu psyche, which persist till date. This shock-shatter-and-grab encroachment of his holy jihad had, for the first time, created Islam's existence in India as a separate unit, which, unlike alien populations of the

---
[68] Ibid.
[69] Durant, *The Story of Civilization, Volume I: Our Oriental Heritage*, 1,007.

past, never assimilated into the dominant fold of an ancient Dharma rooted in compassion and all-encompassing inclusivity. The generic word, 'Hindu', was introduced perhaps for the first time around this period. But probably, the most lasting damage that Mahmud of Ghazni had inflicted was this: his merciless, serial demolition of temples and *murtis* and everything that Hindus venerated as sacred in his fanatical zeal to establish the Only True Faith in this land of idolaters gave birth to a new pejorative that was universally despised by Hindus: Turushka and its variants—for example, its Kannada variant, Turuka.

After his last-ever campaign against the Jats who had mounted such fierce opposition during his panicked flight from Somanatha, Mahmud contracted malaria. Prolonged medical treatment led to further complications and he contracted fatal tuberculosis in 1030, from which he never recovered.

However, he had opened the floodgates wider for subsequent Islamic conquests because Afghanistan and large portions of Punjab had already been lost to Muslim rule. More importantly, his daring expedition and devastation at distant Somanatha had made him a legendary hero throughout the Muslim world, which saw him as a Ghazi worthy of emulation. Mahmud had shown that mainland Sindh could be successfully penetrated if the true warrior of Islam was equipped with great planning, strategy, ruthlessness and deceit and had unshakeable faith in the 'guiding hand of Allah'. Such a warrior would then be rewarded with assured victories where the blood of the infidels would flow so copiously that the river streams would be discoloured, 'notwithstanding its purity'[70], and the infidels would be unable to drink it. Even the contemporary historian trained

---

[70] Utbi, "Tarikh Yamini," 40–1.

in modern methods of scholarship and historiography, Muhammad Nazim, cannot hide his admiration for Mahmud of Ghazni, 'the magnificent thief'[71], who had so savagely destroyed Somanatha. In Nazim's own words, 'The idol of Somnath itself perished but it immortalised the name of Sultan Mahmud.'[72]

As we've seen earlier, fantastic tales and legends were woven around Mahmud's exploits. Even during his final days, he had become some sort of a mythical figure, feared and revered in the annals of holy Islamic conquerors and glorified by Muslim saints and Sufis and Pirs. Over time, generations of Muslim chroniclers, hagiographers and holy men built up a huge literary corpus[73] eulogising Mahmud.

Mahmud's son, Masu'd I erected an opulent mausoleum over the tomb of his father to honour his memory as a pioneering warrior of Islam. He decreed rich endowments for its maintenance. For centuries, Mahmud's tomb became a magnet attracting a wide range of people: military adventurers who aspired to follow his pious path, Sunni saints, poets and random admirers. All of them believed that they would be blessed with Allah's grace by paying obeisance to it. Each such seeker would take away some fragment from the monument: pieces of wood and chunks of soil and keep it at their homes as a sort of talisman. In 1842, Lord Ellenborough yanked out the gates to this mausoleum, believing them to be the original gates of the Somanatha Temple and carted them off. Today, the gates lie in the Agra Fort, decrepit and decaying.

---

[71] Durant, *The Story of Civilization, Volume I: Our Oriental Heritage*, 1,008.
[72] Nazim, *The Life and Times of Sultan Mahmud of Ghazna*, 120–1.
[73] For example, Wasaya-i-Nizamu'l-Mulk, Mantiqu't-Tair and Futuh's-Salatin. For a fuller list, see "Appendix M," in Nazim, *The Life and Times of Sultan Mahmud of Ghazna*.

CHAPTER 3

The Civilisational Cost of Misplaced Magnanimity

The land of Ajmer, soaked with the blood of the Turushkas, looked as if it had dressed itself in a dress of deep red colour to celebrate the victory of her lord.
                              An inscription at the Ajmer Museum[1]

Until the Mughals, none of the Muslim dynasties in India had regimes outlasting the prestige, power and magnitude achieved under its greatest emperor. A significant reason for this lies in the manner in which succession was decided in the Islamic system of statecraft. As long as the sultan was ruling and alive, he permitted no one, not even his own sons, to wield even a semblance of political decisiveness. Succession was chiefly decided either on the sultan's deathbed or when he had irreversibly declined in physical or mental faculties. Or in most typical cases, succession was decided purely on the sultan's whim. Even so, when the successor ascended the throne, there was no guarantee of loyalty or stability ... or his life itself. It was a savage tribal system where the most ruthless of them took it all and kept it with him as long as he was alive. Even a veneer of challenge to his absolute despotism would be quelled mercilessly. Mahmud of Ghazni is himself the most representative specimen of this system. The manner in which he usurped the throne at Ghazni presents an early and classic case. With a shrewd

---
[1] This is a Chauhan *prasasti* (inscription) of Ajmer Museum, line 15.

behind-the-scenes alliance with his other brother, Abu'l-Muzaffar, he had deposed his younger brother Ismail who had been anointed as the successor by Sabuktigin. One of the most incisive and brilliant commentaries on this primitive, tribal system of succession notes:

> [T]he sultans never divided the succession of the kingdom; nor did they designate a successor. All sons were groomed to rule, but only one could take the throne – *a method that seemed brutally designed to ensure the survival of the fittest. Most startling of all … they paid no attention to succession through marriage.* Where emperors [in other nations] … went to exhaustive lengths to secure dynastic marriages and legitimate succession through approved bloodlines, the [sultans] hardly bothered. *A sultan's father would naturally be the previous sultan, but his mother might be a concubine or a slave, possibly not a born Muslim, and from one of a dozen subject peoples* [emphases added].[2]

From one perspective, it can be said that the entire history of the medieval Muslim dynasties of India is just one sweeping kaleidoscope of violent and incessant palace intrigues, brutal fratricides and patricides, and interminable rebellions solely aimed at capturing despotic imperial power.

Raja Dharma

The contrast with the great Hindu dynasties from the ancient times cannot be more pronounced. Barring a handful of exceptions, dynastic succession was generally smooth and vetted and accepted by everyone in accordance with the tenets of both Raja Dharma[3] and Kshatriya Dharma.

---

[2] Crowley, 1453: The Holy War for Constantinople and the Clash of Islam and the *West*, 36–7.
[3] For an exhaustive discussion, see 'The Tradition of Kshatra in India', *Prekshaa Journal*.

Hindu political philosophy lays great emphasis on the personal character and conduct of the ruler who was, most of all, anxious about the acceptance of his suzerainty by the majority of, if not the entire, citizenry. This in turn emerges from the same political philosophy which ordains that the king should always strive to earn the goodwill and *affection* of his subjects. It also enjoins the people to overthrow any king who concentrates absolute power in himself. The earliest example of this precept in action is the fabled account of Chanakya who deposed Dhanananda and installed Chandragupta Maurya, a brave and capable youth of humble origins, on the throne of the Magadha Empire. This inbuilt quality of bloodless succession can most notably be seen in the vast, Dharmic empires of the Mauryas, Shatavahanas, Guptas, Pallavas, Vakatakas, Cholas, Chalukyas, Palas, Gurjara-Pratiharas, Hoysalas, Rashtrakutas, Paramaras, and the grand Vijayanagara dynasties, roughly spanning an awe-inspiring period of more than a millennium. Against the vast canvas of the history of human political organisation, this prolonged and unbroken record of India holds a high distinction as one of the unparalleled examples of entirely homegrown political genius. The same innate quality also ensured extraordinary durability, stability and unbroken continuity of these empires. It was also a great catalyst that tempered unruly passions motivated by inordinate political ambition in the larger political climate. These core civilisational elements, among others, are what birthed the grand works of Hindu art, architecture and sculpture, most of which have an inherently meditative quality.

The Ghaznavid Empire implodes

Growing up under the looming banyan-shadow of Mahmud of Ghazni obviously had a deleterious and weakening impact on his son and successor, Mas'ud I. In just seven years after Mahmud's death, the Seljuk Turks under the leadership of Tughril, overwhelmed and sacked Ghazni itself. By 1040, Mas'ud I abandoned almost all of his western territories to the Seljuks and fled to India. In the same year, his own army revolted against him and installed his brother Mohammad on the throne. Mohammad wasted no time in imprisoning and then executing him. After Mohammad's death, the remnants of the Ghaznavid Empire were ruled by a series of weak and worthless kings, only in name. By 1115, the mighty empire of Mahmud of Ghazni had been reduced to the feeble status of a vassal and a protectorate of the Seljuk Turks. Even this did not last long. In 1141, the Central Asian marauder, Gur Khan of the Qara Khitai Turkish stock, devastated the Seljuks beyond recovery.

Two new powers emerged from the ashes of this devastation: the Khwarazm Shahs and the Ghurids (also known as Ghors and Ghurs). Both feasted on the carcass of the Ghaznavid Empire, and the latter sowed the seeds of the first Muslim empire in mainland India.

The House of Ghor

The rise of the chiefs of Ghor[4] is one of the eccentric accidents of history, given their unspecific origins in the remote, treacherous and inaccessible region of central Afghanistan 'bounded by the districts of Herat, Farrah, Dawar, Rabat, Kurwan, and Gharjistan'[5]. For scores of centuries, it had been the perfect location for Buddhist monks who had made it their home to live a life of secluded contemplation inside its caves. The Muslim chroniclers al-Istakhri and Ibn Haukal record that when Mahmud of Ghazni invaded Ghor

---

[4] Now in the Hazarajat region of Afghanistan.
[5] Elliot and Dowson, *The History of India as Told by Its Own Historians*, Vol. 2, 576.

in 1011, it was still 'a country of infidels, containing only a few Musulmans, and the inhabitants spoke a language different from that of Khurasan'[6]. In remaining true to his religious piety, Mahmud converted[7] a significant portion of its population to Islam. He also left behind the ulema or the Islamic clergy to more fully instruct[8] the Ghors or Ghurids about the glories of Islam. Yet the infidels were stubborn and the 'extension of Islam and its cultural institutions, and the conversion of Ghōr, took a long time. As late as the end of the tenth century, the population of Ghōr was for the most part heathen. According to al-Istakharı, '*it was the biggest pagan enclave within the borders of Islam* [emphasis added].'[9]

More than a century after Mahmud's death, two Ghurid brothers emerged after being freed from the dreary confines of a prison in a fortress in Wahiristan[10]. Their ancestors had been Buddhists but they had no generational memory of it. Around 1160–1161, they had been thrown into prison by their own uncle, the 'world-burner'[11], the self-styled 'sultan' Ala-ud-din Husain, who had marched against Bahram Shah, one of Mahmud of Ghazni's last descendants, and sacked and burnt the city of Ghazni to the last atom, except the grand mausoleum erected in the honour of Mahmud.

---

[6] Ibid.
[7] John McLeod, *The History of India* (California: Greenwood Publishing Group, 2002), 34.
[8] Satish Chandra, *Medieval India: From Sultanat to the Mughals–Delhi Sultanat (1206–1526)* (New Delhi: Har Anand Publications, 2007), 22.
[9] K.A. Nizami, *History of Civilizations of Central Asia*, Vol.4, Part 1 (Paris: UNESCO Publications, 1994), 183.
[10] It is unclear which place this corresponds to in the modern time.
[11] Ala-ud-din Husain was known as *Jahansuz* (world-burner) because he subjected Ghazni to seven days of non-stop ransacking, plunder and genocide, killing sixty thousand of its inhabitants. All the tombs of the Ghaznavid rulers, except those of Mahmud (of Ghazni), Mas'ud and Ibrahim, were broken open and the remains burned. See "Ala-al-din Hosayn Jahansuz," in *Encyclopaedia Iranica*, online edition, accessed on 20 September 2016, http://www.iranicaonline.org/articles/ala-al-din-hosayn-b

The crime of the two brothers—after this 'world-burner' had sacked Ghazni, he had appointed them at the head of a province called Sunja[12], and with their newfound power, the brothers quickly began raiding the neighbouring territories without their uncle's permission. The enraged uncle sent a contingent against them and flung them into the aforementioned prison.

However, after Ala-ud-din Husain's death in 1161, his son Sayf al-Din Muhammad freed his cousins. And then, in just two years, fortune lavished a generous smile upon them: in 1163, Sayf died in a battle against the Oghuz Turks. His elder cousin, the older of the two pardoned brothers, Ghiyath al-Din Muhammad ascended the throne of Ghor.

Ghiyath al-Din Muhammad's younger brother was Shihab-ud-din Muhammad, alias Mu'izz ad-Din Muhammad bin Sam, infamously etched in the Indian historical consciousness as Muhammad of Ghori, who ultimately won the history-altering battle because his formidable enemy Prithviraja Chahamana or Prithviraj Chauhan had lost sight of the civilisational cost of the generosity he had shown to this perfidious foe.

There was a fundamental reason his 'world-burner' uncle Ala-ud-din Husain had spared the tomb of Mahmud of Ghazni. Mahmud, through his pious deeds, had stamped his position in the Muslim world as the hero and role model[13] of every Muslim soldier and aspiring conqueror. Entirely consistent with this tradition, Muhammad of Ghori, too, said an earnest prayer[14] to Mahmud of Ghazni, the pioneering Ghazi who had paved the way to plunder

---

[12] This is the name of the place given by Firishta. However, as Briggs says, it is unclear what this place corresponds to in the modern time. (Briggs, *History of the Rise of the Mahomedan Power in India till the Year A.D. 1612*, Vol. 1, 167–8.)

[13] K.S. Lal, *The Legacy of Muslim Rule in India* (New Delhi: Voice of India, 1992).

[14] Majumdar, *The History and Culture of the Indian People*, Vol. 5, 117.

Hind and plant the victorious flag of the Faith in this land of idolaters and untold wealth, beseeching him to give him the strength to emulate his exploits.

Humiliated by a boy

By the time Muhammad of Ghori had turned in the direction of mainland India, the situation had dramatically altered from the time of Mahmud of Ghazni. The political configuration had witnessed sweeping changes, and the Hindus had recouped and renewed their strength, and Muhammad would learn, repeatedly and at an enormous cost, that he was no match for them.

When he marched in the direction of Gujarat in 1178, a series of disastrous humiliations was waiting for him around every corner.

That year marked, roughly, five hundred and forty years of successive and repeated attempts by the Islamic armies of the Arabs and the Turks to establish even a foothold in the heartland of India and implant the message of the Only True Faith here. So far, they had succeeded only in occupying the frontier areas of Kabul, Zabul, the North-West Frontier Province, Multan and parts of Punjab and Sindh.

By all accounts, Muhammad of Ghori was vastly inferior to his more daring predecessor in valour, striking power and military acumen in spite of the fact that he now possessed a distinct advantage that Mahmud of Ghazni hadn't: a fairly detailed knowledge of India—its geography, routes, cities, political set-up and culture as well as the Hindu religion and society. Al-Biruni's *India* and Burhanuddin's *al-Hidaya*, apart from numerous oral accounts by contemporary Muslim chroniclers, supplied this much-needed knowledge.

However, in his hasty zeal to emulate his more illustrious predecessor Mahmud, he had forgotten to study, remember or learn valuable lessons from Mahmud's greatest failure on his 'victorious' return journey to Ghazni via the Sindh desert. Muhammad of Ghori was impatiently salivating at the prospect of replicating the pious performance of Mahmud in Somanatha with greater success and effectiveness. The glowing accounts of Somanatha's devastation recorded so colourfully by Muslim chroniclers and the high status that Mahmud had earned in the eyes of the Caliph had fuelled Muhammad's fantasies of an easy conquest. What he had also overlooked was the fact that a full one hundred and fifty years had elapsed in the interim; Gujarat was now more powerful than before. But impatient and incredibly thirsty with ambition, Muhammad marched against the dictates of geography with a large army, taking the route of the treacherous Thar desert in western Rajasthan. Towards Anhilwara. However, when he reached the foothills of Mount Abu with a famished and exhausted army, he found that his massive force was thoroughly unprepared for what he faced: a determined army of infidels led by a mere boy, the (eventual) Gujarat Chalukya king, Mularaja II. His mother, Queen Nayakadevi[15] pitched the boy in this battle against the reviled Turushkas, leading from the front. At Gadaraghatta[16], the armies of the 'Mahomedans' were defeated with great slaughter'[17] and Muhammad himself managed to escape after 'suffer[ing] many hardships in their retreat to Ghazni'.[18] It was a mortal blow to Muhammad's confidence when he surveyed the battered ruins of his

---

[15] Daughter of the Goan Kadamba ruler, Mahamandalesvara Paramardin, and the widow of Gujarat Chalukya king, Ajaya Pala.
[16] Battle of Kasahrada near modern-day Kyara in Sirohi district, Gujarat.
[17] Elliot and Dowson, *The History of India as Told by Its Own Historians*, Vol. 2, 294.
[18] Briggs, *History of the Rise of the Mahomedan Power in India till the Year A.D. 1612*, 170.

surviving army. For the next twelve years, he did not lead a single expedition against any Hindu ruler.

The victory against the Turushkas was deservedly celebrated in the annals[19] of Gujarat's historical memory by an impressive array of poets and in inscriptions of the era. Sanskrit inscriptions in Gujarat record that Mularaja II was the conqueror of the Garjanakas (dwellers of Ghazni). An inscription by Bhimadeva II[20] reads:

> Even a woman could defeat the Hammira [Amir], during the reign of Mulraja II.

A taste of Prithviraja's valour

When Muhammad of Ghori led the expedition after twelve years, he was routed even more severely, notwithstanding the fact that he had amassed greater resources and territories in the interim. During the same interval, Muhammad had raided and taken Peshawar in 1178, Sialkot in 1185 and Lahore in 1186. Khusrav Malik, the ruler of Lahore, was the last shard in the millions of shattered pieces that the Ghaznavid dynasty had now become. Minhaju-s Siraj encapsulates the extinction of the Ghaznavid dynasty with a tinge of melodrama in his poetry:

> The house of Mahmud had now come to its end;
> the sun of its glory was set,
> the registrar of fate had written
> the mandate of its destruction.[21]

---

[19] Examples include the work of Someshwara, the court poet of the Chalukyas of Gujarat; *Prabandha Chintamani* of the Jain poet Acharya Merutunga; the poet Balachandra; and *Sukrita-Kirti-Kallolini* of Udayaprabha Suri.

[20] Brother and successor of Mularaja II.

[21] Minhaju-s Siraj, "Tabaqat-i-Nasiri," in *The History of India as Told by Its Own Historians*, Vol. 2, 294.

With the capture of these three key cities, Punjab was now under the sway of Muhammad. Almost. He was now knocking at the borders of the kingdom of the mighty Chahamana, Prithviraja III of Ajmer.

Prithviraja III was still a minor when he was coronated to the throne of Ajayameru or Ajmer. His mother, Queen Karpuradevi, ruled as the regent and vastly improved and beautified Ajmer with parks, gardens and wells. It enjoyed enviable prosperity. In 1178, Prithviraja took full control of the kingdom and eventually, began a series of expeditions and consolidations that made the Chahamana Empire a formidable force, stretching across Rajasthan, parts of Gujarat, Delhi, Bundelkhand and the Gahadawala kingdom centred in Kanauj. One of the greatest strengths that aided Prithviraja was the close circle of able, competent and extremely loyal advisors and officers such as Kadambavasa, Bhuvanaikamalla, Sodha, Skanda and Vamana. However, almost immediately after taking charge, he was confronted with danger in the form of the selfsame Muhammad of Ghori who was en route to his disastrous campaign against Gujarat. Muhammad had learnt that Prithviraja had an inveterate hatred towards the Turushkas who had ravaged and desecrated the sacred land of Bharatavarsha on countless occasions without reason. In a bid at making an opportunistic alliance, Muhammad sent a diplomatic mission to Prithviraja, which failed miserably. Enraged, Muhammad decided to provoke him. At Kiradu near Barmer, he plundered and vandalised the Someshwara Temple and captured Nadol, which was the capital of a branch of the Chahamana bloodline. As anticipated, an inflamed Prithviraja resolved to punish Muhammad but was stopped by the wise counsel of Kadambavasa: give Muhammad a long

THE COST OF MISPLACED MAGNANIMITY 93

rope. Let him exhaust himself. And then we'll see what to do next. Kadambavasa was proven right. Soon, a messenger arrived at his court from Gujarat with good news: the boy Mularaja II had pounded Muhammad. Prithviraja lavished gifts on the messenger. And on his wise minister.

At any rate, by the time Muhammad of Ghori had returned after the twelve-year-long hiatus, Prithviraja Chahamana's empire encompassed a vast swathe of territory: up to Hissar and Sirhind in the northwest, Delhi in the north, Mewar as the southern border, Bayana, Gwalior and Gahadawala in the east. While he had inherited most of these, he had also acquired a few on his own.

Emboldened by these important victories at Peshawar, Sialkot and Lahore, Muhammad almost immediately launched a series of destructive raids into some minor territories of Prithviraja Chahamana. When he found success, his confidence was restored. He would no longer face the same humiliation that he had suffered in Gujarat. On the contrary, Muhammad was now set to conquer all of Hindustan. He led a large force, stormed and captured the fortress of Sirhind (Tabarhindah in Muslim chronicles) right inside Prithviraja's territory. He appointed Malik Ziya-ud-din as its in-charge and appointed twelve hundred horsemen to hold it for eight months. He said he had to return to Ghazni on some urgent work. The impetuous capture of Sirhind was a direct taunt to Prithviraja, who either took it rather lightly or wasn't fully updated about the danger this posed. His feudatories didn't. A few weeks later, Chandraraja visited the Chahamana at Ajmer in person with this report.

> The beef-eating Mleccha, Shihab-ud-din has pillaged and burnt most of our cities, defiled our women and has reduced them to a miserable plight. There is scarcely a mountain-pent valley in which his brutal tyranny has not

suffocated the noblest of Rajputs who have fled here for protection from him. Scores of these noble Rajput families have disappeared before him and he has now established his capital at Multan. He is an unrelenting enemy.[22]

Chandraraja was the son of Govindaraja, the governor of Delhi and trusted vassal of Prithviraja. He was accompanied by other feudatories. When Prithviraja heard this shocking report, he decided that it was time to punish Muhammad. Accordingly, he set out at the head of a massive force of two lakh horsemen and three thousand elephants. Muhammad, still in Sirhind, was taken completely by surprise at Prithviraja's swiftness. He abandoned his travel plans and quickly pulled up his troops.

In 1191, the foes met at the historic site of Tarain, just 80 miles from Delhi.[23] From the beginning, it was an uneven battle and it didn't take long for Prithviraja to outflank, outnumber and shatter Muhammad's army. Its right and left wings broke apart under the Chahamana's onslaught and its central division, too, quickly began losing numbers and courage. However, still intoxicated with the successful capture of the Sirhind Fort, Muhammad was blissfully oblivious to this frontal disaster occurring right before his own eyes and refused to heed his informant's advice to retreat. Instead, he chose to rush in where angels feared to tread. Unsheathing his sword, he charged forward against the superior enemy. When Govindaraja spotted this, he rushed at him with extraordinary speed, seated on his battle-trained elephant. However, Muhammad was quick to react and threw a spear at Govindaraja, knocking off 'two of the accursed wretch's

---

[22] Majumdar, *The History and Culture of the Indian People*, Vol. 5, 110.
[23] Muslim chroniclers give the name as Narain. This can be identified as the modern-day Tarori in Haryana, just 14 miles from Thanesar and 80 miles from Delhi.

teeth down his throat'. Undaunted, Govindaraja returned the favour by hurling a javelin with such force that it caused a pothole-like wound in Muhammad's arm, the blood gushing out like a fountain. The impact of Govindaraja's deadly projectile threw Muhammad off his horse, the agony of the fresh wound so unbearable that he could no longer hold the reins. Just as he was falling, a trusted foot soldier of the Khalji Turkish stock sprang with 'lightning speed' to his rescue, hauled him on a horse and clasping Muhammad to his bosom, sped away to safety. But for this great fortune, Muhammad would have bled to death on the battlefield. Firishta calls[24] this assistance as a 'triumph', one that includes blaming Muhammad's army for 'wholly' deserting him. However, Minhaju-s Siraj extols Muhammad as a 'second Rustam and the Lion of the Age'.[25] However, the battle was far from over. Siraj narrates what happened next.

> When the Musulmans lost sight of the sultan, a panic fell upon them; they fled and halted not until they were safe from the pursuit of the victors. A party of nobles and youths of Ghor had seen and recognized their leader with that lion-hearted Khilji, and when he came up they drew together, and, forming a kind of litter with broken lances, they bore him to the halting place. *The hearts of the troops were consoled by his appearance, and the Muhammadan faith gathered new strength in his life. He collected the scattered forces and retreated to the territories of Islam, leaving Kazi Tolak in the fort of Sarhind* [Sirhind] [emphasis added].[26]

Prithviraja's victorious troops pursued Muhammad for forty miles before returning. Now it was left to the hapless Malik

---
[24] Briggs, *History of the Rise of the Mahomedan Power in India till the Year A.D. 1612*, Vol. 1, 173.
[25] Elliot and Dowson, *The History of India as Told by Its Own Historians*, Vol. 2, 296.
[26] Ibid.

Ziya-ud-din alias Kazi Tolak to defend himself all alone at the Sirhind Fort. He surrendered after a prolonged siege lasting thirteen months. Prithviraja Chahamana had wrested back the control of Punjab.

'Recover my lost honour from those idolaters!'

Meanwhile at Ghor, the twice-humiliated Muhammad was busy inflicting his fury on the officers and nobles who had abandoned him at Tarain. He rounded them up in full public view, gathered the 'mouth-bags' of their own respective horses, filled them with raw barley, slung these weighty bags around their necks and made them walk around the city, forcing them at sword point to eat the raw barley grain 'like brutes'. Then he threw them all in prison as punishment for this 'stain on their character'.[27]

Then he also made a solemn vow to himself:

> Since the time of my defeat in Hindustan, I have never slumbered in ease, or waked, but in sorrow and anxiety. I have, therefore, determined, with this army, to recover my lost honour from those idolaters, or die in the attempt.[28]

By the next year, Muhmmad marched to the same Tarain with a massive force of one lakh twenty thousand armoured horsemen drawn from an assortment of Turks, Afghans and Khokars. He arrived at Tarain via Peshawar, Multan and Lahore. From Lahore, he sent a message to Prithviraja at Ajmer through his emissary, Rukn-u-ddin Hamza: 'embrace the True Muhammadan faith and acknowledge my supremacy. Your refusal to do so will be treated as a

---

[27] Ibid., 174.
[28] Ibid.

declaration of war.'²⁹ Prithviraja Chahamana called his bluff and sent his reply in the language it deserved:

> To the bravery of our soldiers we believe you are no stranger, and to our great superiority in numbers which daily increases, your eyes bear witness. You will repent in time of the rash resolution you have taken, and we shall permit you to retreat in safety; but if you have determined to brave your destiny, we have sworn by our gods to advance upon you with our rank-breaking elephants, our plain-trampling horses, and blood-thirsty soldiers, early in the morning to crush the army which your ambition has led to ruin.³⁰

Unlike the previous year, Muhammad of Ghori replaced bravado with perfidy and lulled Prithviraja into a false sense of peace by claiming that he had come to make truce according to the orders of his elder brother, Ghiyath al-Din Muhammad. Prithviraja naively believed him and lowered his guard. In the opaque wall of darkness before the next fateful morning of 1192, Muhammad of Ghori rudely, unexpectedly sprung the Second Battle of Tarain. It is unnecessary to narrate the detailed tale of this well-known watershed battle in Indian history of which copious[31] accounts exist. Muhammad of Ghori won it through sheer treachery, not valour.

---

[29] Majumdar, *The History and Culture of the Indian People*, Vol. 5, 111.
[30] Firishta, "Tarikh-i Firishta", quoted verbatim in Goel, *Heroic Hindu Resistance to Muslim Invaders (636 AD to 1206 AD)*, 22.
[31] Well-known Indian sources include *Viruddhavidhi-viddhavamsa, Prabandha Chintamani, Hammira Mahakavya* and *Prithviraj Raso*. Notable Muslim histories include *Jamiu-l Hikayath, Taju-l Ma'asir, Tabaqat-i-Nasiri* and *Tabaqat-i-Akbari*. For insightful discussions about both battles of Tarain, the following sources may be consulted: (1) Majumdar, *The History and Culture of the Indian People*, Vol. 5; (2) Goel, *Heroic Hindu Resistance to Muslim Invaders (636 AD to 1206 AD)*; (3) Misra, *Indian Resistance to Muslim Invaders up to 1206 A.D.*; (4) Dasharatha Sharma, *Early Chauhan Dynasties* (New Delhi: Motilal Banarsidass Publishers, 1975); and (5) Cynthia Talbot, *The Last Hindu Emperor: Prithviraj Chauhan and the Indian Past, 1200–2000* (Cambridge: Cambridge University Press, 2016).

Prithviraja Chahamana was beheaded and died perhaps without realising the civilisational cost of his misplaced magnanimity. The respected historian and first-rate scholar D.C. Ganguly presents a pithy but melancholic analysis of this cost.

> Prithviraja was evidently a general of high order, but he lacked political foresight. It was a grave defect with the Indian chiefs that in their fight with the Muslims they always chose to be on the defensive. The result was that their adversaries, even when they were defeated, could escape annihilation if they could only withdraw from the battlefield. Prithviraja was not free from this drawback. At this time the rule of the Maliks of Ghur was not firmly established in the Punjab. Prithviraja ought to have pursued the disabled Sultan … after his victory in the first battle of Tarain, and made an attempt to root out the Muslim rule there.… The defeat of Prithviraja in the second battle of Tarain not only destroyed the imperial power of the Chahamanas, but also brought disaster on the whole of Hindustan. The morale of the ruling princes and the people completely broke down, and the entire country was seized with panic.[32]

The civilisational significance of the battle of Tarain is also couched in another profound facet: Tarain is just about 25 km from Kurukshetra, the grand theatre of the Mahabharata war where Dharma had triumphed over *adharma*.

The last Hindu emperor of Bharatavarsha had died and with him, her independence.

---

[32] Majumdar, *The History and Culture of the Indian People,*, Vol. 5, 113.

Creation of the *zimmis*

The decisive victory of Muhammad of Ghori was also the harbinger of several permanent firsts in India, as we shall see later in this book.

It marks the first episode of forced and panicked mass migrations of Hindus, Jains and other native non-Muslim populations from various parts of northern and western India towards the central and southern regions. Indeed, a separate volume dedicated to narrating the full history of such forced Hindu migrations within India awaits the pen of a future historian. One of the more enduring and durable features of Hindu social life since time immemorial was the remarkable continuity and attachment they had towards their immediate geographical surroundings. Muhammad's perfidious victory shattered that sense of permanence and continuity forever. From then onwards, this age-old stability and settled generational rhythm of life would repeatedly be smashed for the next five hundred years throughout northern, eastern and western India by the same forces of religious zealotry and iconoclasm that motivated Muhammad bin Qasim, Mahmud of Ghazni and now, Muhammad of Ghori. The Jain Acharya Asadhara writes[33] that when the Sapadalaksha[34] region was conquered by Shihab-ud-din alias Muhammad of Ghor, he fled from his native country and migrated to the safe haven of Malwa, because he was scared of being forcibly converted and his family molested by the marauding armies.

The other tragic precedent that ensued in the wake of Muhammad's victory was that for the first time, Hindus in mainland India got a new identity, which would continue till

---

[33] Ibid., 113.
[34] Roughly corresponds to present-day Sambhar Lake Town, also historically known as Shakambhari.

the collapse of the Mughal Empire: *zimmi*, or *dhimmi*. The later-day Sufi saint Amir Khusrow Dehlavi, better known as Amir Khusrav, delineates the full, pious import of the term:

> Happy Hindustan, the splendour of Religion, where the Law finds perfect honour and security. The whole country, by means of the sword of our holy warriors, has become like a forest denuded of its thorns by fire. *Islam is triumphant, idolatry is subdued. Had not the Law granted exemption from death by the payment of poll-tax, the very name of Hind, root and branch, would have been extinguished* [emphasis added].[35]

Flushed with the decisive victory over Prithviraja Chahamana, Muhammad marched into Ajmer, captured it, slaughtered thousands of its inhabitants who had dared to oppose him, and 'reserved the rest for slavery'[36]. Scores of 'idol temples' were demolished, and the famous Sanskrit college of Vigraharaja IV was converted into a mosque. Hasan Nizami is ecstatic.

> The victorious army on the right and on the left departed towards Ajmer. When the crow-faced Hindus began to sound their white shells on the backs of the elephants, you would have said that a river of pitch was flowing impetuously down the face of a mountain of blue. The army of Islam was completely victorious, and a hundred thousand grovelling Hindus swiftly departed to the fire of hell. He destroyed (at Ajmer) the pillars and foundations of the idol temples, and built in their stead mosques and colleges, and the precepts

---

[35] Quoted in Lal, *The Legacy of Muslim Rule in India*, 53.
[36] Briggs, *History of the Rise of the Mahomedan Power in India till the Year A.D. 1612*, Vol. I, 177.

of Islam, and the customs of the law were divulged and established.³⁷

Next, Muhammad marched to Delhi and inflicted a similar horror on the 'Rai' who had dared to invite the 'dread of [Muhammad's] punishment'³⁸. A 'torrent of blood flowed on the battle' but the badly outnumbered Hindu governor had to eventually surrender and 'placed his head upon the line of slavery'.

The conquest of Hindustan, at least in his mind, was now complete, and he finally set out for Ghazni.

Death by twenty-two cuts

However, Muhammad would not live long to peacefully enjoy the spoils of his rampage and plunder. In less than ten years, his empire on the other side of Hindustan was fast imploding. His old foes, the Khwarezmians had snatched even Herat from the Ghurids. In 1202, his elder brother, Ghiyath al-Din died, and Muhammad became the sultan of the Ghurid Empire. In 1204, he himself suffered a massive defeat at Andkhud³⁹ at the hands of the selfsame Khwarezmians led by Muhammad II from which he never recovered. It was a degrading, personal humiliation more than an actual military defeat. Hopelessly cornered, his life was spared only after he paid a hefty ransom to the accursed upstart. This incident had predictable consequences.

In less than a year, revolts erupted like wildfire across his dominions in northwestern India. The Khokhars and numerous other unnamed tribes blazed across the region, reached Multan

---

[37] Hasan Nizami, "Taju-l Ma'asir," in *The History of India as Told by Its Own Historians*, Vol. 2, 214–15.
[38] Ibid.
[39] Present-day Andkhoy in northwestern Afghanistan.

and captured its governor. Next, they plundered Lahore itself and shut the road between Lahore and Ghazni. The work of Muhammad's entire life was coming apart before his own eyes like the threads of a fine royal garment. Yet, he was hopelessly desperate to stitch them back and personally marched to the newly usurped region, and in a vicious battle that lasted five months between the Jhelum and the Chenab rivers, he finally defeated and slaughtered the Khokhars with extraordinary cruelty. He reoccupied Lahore on 25 February 1206 and brought a semblance of normalcy and headed back to Ghazni.

Eighteen days later, when he was sleeping in his tent at night at a place called Damyak on the bank of the Vedic Sindhu River, two Khokhar avengers barged in and 'without hesitation, sheathed their daggers in the King's body, which was afterwards found to have been pierced by no fewer than 22 wounds'.[40]

Muhammad's body was carried to Ghazni and buried there.

Muhammad of Ghori did not have a son and successor. The Ghurid dynasty was extinguished.[41]

However, what he had left behind in Hindustan in the aftermath of his devastating incursions proved far more enduring.

Instead of leaving behind a son, he had left behind a pack of slaves.

Before departing to Ghazni in 1192–1193, Muhammad of Ghori had stationed one of his favourite slaves, who originally

---

[40] Briggs, *History of the Rise of the Mahomedan Power in India till the Year A.D. 1612*, Vol. 1, 185–6.

[41] The extinction took a few years. Ghiyath al-Din's son and Muhammad Ghori's nephew, Mahmud ascended to the throne at Ghor. But the empire he had inherited had shattered beyond repair. He became a quasi-vassal of the Khwarezmian Shah and died soon after.

hailed from Turkestan, at Indarpat or Indraprastha, about 10 miles from Delhi. His name was Qutb al-Din Aybeg or Qutub-ud-din Aibak, and he had long since been elevated to the rank of a general. Aibak had been vested with the command of a good chunk of Muhammad's army and appointed[42] as the chief in-charge of all territories conquered by Muhammad in Hindustan. While Aibak lacked the valour, ruthlessness and resources of Muhammad, he overcompensated with shrewdness, trickery and foresight by gradually cutting off ties with the Turkic Muslim empires in Central Asia.

On 26 June 1206, four safe months after Muhammad's brutal end, Qutub-ud-din Aibak assumed the supreme power at Lahore.

―――・・◆・・―――

With it, the first Turkish Muslim sultanate was established in Hindustan, and for the first time in the history of India's ancient civilisation, the seeds were sown for the concentration of absolute, despotic political power that had the unstinted backing of an Islamic clergy, which in turn derived its authority from scripture. This was a political phenomenon India had never witnessed before, and which would irreversibly alter the destiny of this ancient civilisation for the worse. The Classical Age which had disappeared forever in the previous century would now be replaced by a form of oppressive imperial barbarism, which would find, again, scriptural justification for its oppression. If none was found, the despot's ever-ready iron hand would do the needful. It is a legacy whose vestiges continue till date.

―――・・◆・・―――

---

[42] For a fuller discussion on the exact circumstances of this appointment, see Peter Jackson, *The Delhi Sultanate: A Political and Military History* (New York: Cambridge University Press, 2003), 26 onwards.

CHAPTER 4

A Sultanate of Turkic Slaves

We came down on them like a flood!
We went out among their cities!
We tore down the idol-temples,
We shat on the Buddha's head![1]

　　　　　　　　　　　Mahmud al-Kashgari

The shattered octogenarian sultan lay on his deathbed, incoherent but desperate to install his own bloodline on the throne of Delhi, one who would continue his glorious legacy as the pious king whose heart was the repository of Allah's favour[2] and in this aspect, he didn't have an equal in all of mankind. Since ascending the throne of Delhi twenty years ago, he had taken this calling of the heart seriously, gravely even. He had been entrusted the lieutenancy of the *khilafat* or the *niyabat*—the lieutenancy[3] of Allah himself on this earth—when he had enthroned himself as sultan, titling himself Ghiyas-ud-din Balban after his weak, vacillating and ineffective son-in-law Nasir-ud-din Mahmud had died in 1265–1266. As a devout Sunni Muslim entrusted with the sultanate, he had done everything according to the Holy Quran and was guided by the wise counsel of the ulema and the Divines with whom he always took his meals. They enlightened him about

---
[1] Mahmud al-Kashgari, quoted in Valerie Hansen, *The Silk Road: A New History* (New York: Oxford University Press, 2012), 228.
[2] A.L. Srivastava, *The Sultanate of Delhi* (Agra: Shiva Lala Agarwala & Company, 1966), 115; For the full text, see Briggs, *History of the Rise of the Mahomedan Power in India till the Year A.D. 1612*, Vol. I, 266–8.
[3] Jackson, *The Delhi Sultanate: A Political and Military History*, 54.

the finer points of Sharia, the Islamic law, and the nuances hidden within the Holy Quran. He had permitted no heresy and had crushed the accursed Ismailis mercilessly and showed the idolaters their true place by breaking their idol temples and strictly enforcing the commands of the Sharia, the Supreme Law, against the *zimmis*—the conquered infidels who had been permitted to still exist as infidels in their own land because there were simply too many of them to slaughter or convince to accept the Light of Islam. Indeed, Balban had done everything according to the word of God throughout his life but fate had dealt him this cruel hand of misery at this late age.

The shattering had occurred exactly a year ago with the untimely murder of his capable and beloved son Muhammad[4] at the hands of the accursed Mongols who had lulled this brave boy with their treachery and massacred most of his army on the banks of the river at Lahore. But *he* was Sultan Ghiyas-ud-din Balban who couldn't afford to display weakness and fallibility. Outwardly, nothing changed. His sternness was intact, his grip over administration unimpaired. It appeared as if nothing had happened. However, in the vast and lonely confines of his royal chamber, he wept bitterly each night. And each passing day only increased the foreboding that his end was near. His second son, the irresponsible and pleasure-loving wretch Bughra Khan, had run away to Lakhnavati[5] unheeding his aged father's pleas to be with him during

---

[4] For the full account, see Briggs, *History of the Rise of the Mahomedan Power in India till the Year A.D. 1612*, Vol. 1, 267–70.

[5] This ancient political and cultural centre known as Gauda has a rich history. It was founded by Shashanka, the illustrious 6th-century ruler of Bengal, and under his regime, the entire region of Bengal became synonymous with Gauda-Desa. Like Shashanka, the Pala and Sena empires which followed him made it their capital. Under the Sena ruler Lakshmanasena, it was renamed as Lakhnavati. The Turkish warlord Bakhtiyar Khalji plundered and destroyed it in 1204. Its ruined remnants are located on the India–Bangladesh border.

his life-ebbing illness. But there was nothing he could do about it. Fast sinking under the 'weight of his affliction', this son's 'undutiful behavior threw the old man into the deepest grief'[6], and he summoned his chief nobles and close friends of several decades: Fakhruddin, the kotwal, and Khwaja Hasan Basri, the wazir, in the early months of 1287. His last will and testament: appoint Kai Khusrav, the son of his beloved son and martyr Muhammad, as his successor. It was also the solemn promise he extracted from them. The courtiers gravely nodded and reaffirmed their loyalty to him even after his death. In reality, the octogenarian's impending death was the golden chance to satisfy their own ravenous hunger, nursed over decades.

Sultan Ghiyas-ud-din Balban's life ended in mid-1287. With it, the train of the Turkic Mamluk slaves who had arrived with Muhammad of Ghori halted forever, after a journey of nearly a century marked by repeated derailments and wreckages too numerous to count.

Balban's death was also the forerunner of an extraordinarily fiendish era, which, for the first time, gave the savage taste of the full range of the horrors of a Muslim invasion south of the Vindhyas, touching the tip of the Indian peninsula.

Disconnecting from Ghazni

Qutub-ud-din Aibak had wasted no time in occupying the seat of power at Lahore in the immediate aftermath of Muhammad's brutal assassination by twenty-two cuts. For a political and pragmatic reason.

Beginning with Mahmud of Ghazni's serial onslaughts into mainland India and his later expansions, Lahore had acted as the southeastern capital of the Ghaznavid territories

---

[6] Briggs, *History of the Rise of the Mahomedan Power in India till the Year A.D. 1612*, Vol. I, 270.

in India. Almost a straight line connected Ghazni with Lahore, making it a key political city from which the Ghaznavids could manage both their northwestern and their Indian territories. Similarly, a short arc could be drawn from Lahore to Delhi via Bhatinda. Lahore was thus the gateway to infidel India. It was also the city that Ghiyath al-Din Muhammad had gifted to his more famous younger brother Muhammad of Ghori to launch his incursions into mainland India. Which is why the latter had made it the capital of his dominions in India. At the height of the Ghaznavid and Ghurid power, Muslim chroniclers[7] had declared Lahore as 'the centre of Islam in India'. Ghaznavid and Ghurid Lahore was a typical Persian city with all its wasteful and unsustainable extravagance built on the blood-soaked foundations of the endless plunder stolen from India. It was where Persian poetry originated and then blossomed and spread to Indian soil as Muslim rule spread deeper in the country. Qutub-ud-din Aibak didn't want a challenger to his newfound power at this strategic power centre.

But the challenger had already reared his head elsewhere. Taj-ud-din Yildiz[8] was a senior peer of Aibak and, like him, Muhammad of Ghori's slave. Muhammad had appointed him as the *Sarwar,* a military commander, a high rank. Taj-ud-din Yildiz was also Aibak's father-in-law. Now, with his boss murdered so brutally in that tent on the banks of the Sindhu River, Yildiz's ambition soared. He had been manumitted[9] by Muhammad of Ghori's weak successor and nephew, Ghiyas-ud-din Mahmud. Yildiz repaid this favour by occupying Ghazni itself. However, the farsighted Aibak

---

[7] For example, the Persian chronicler and author Fakhr-i Mudabbir who provides anecdotes about the rule of Muhammad of Ghori, Qutub-ud-din Aibak and Iltutmish.
[8] Also spelled, Yilduz and Yildoz.
[9] Manumission: The formal freeing of bonded slaves.

had bided his time. Even as Yildiz committed this treachery, Aibak continued to remain loyal to the pleasure-loving Ghiyas-ud-din Mahmud, reading the *Kutba* and minting coins in the name of this namesake sultan, for which he was richly rewarded. In 1208–1209, Ghiyas-ud-din sent him the ceremonial parasol (*chhatra*), and he was free to style himself as the sultan. However, a year earlier, Aibak had already begun to prepare himself for the eventual confrontation with Yildiz. In 1207, he incited some of Yildiz's confidants to stage a palace coup at Ghazni. Concrete details of the outcome of this plot are not known. But Yildiz could not hold on to Ghazni for long. The Khwarezmian Shahs under Ala-ad-din Muhammad were aggressively pushing southwards, and a panicked Yildiz abandoned Ghazni and fled towards Punjab.

Qutub-ud-din Aibak saw his chance. Two birds with one stone. He easily stopped Yildiz in his tracks and prevented him from setting foot in Punjab. Next, he swiftly occupied Ghazni, thereby spoiling the Khwarezmian Shahs' chances. This was perhaps the highest point in his career and he allowed himself to enjoy it to the hilt. Which invariably meant binge drinking and untrammelled debauchery round the clock. With predictable consequences. Firishta writes how the citizens of Ghazni were 'disgusted with his conduct'[10] and sent secret feelers to the selfsame Taj-ud-din Yildiz who was still licking his wounds. These were no ordinary feelers but vivid and precise details of the sultan's habits. And negligence. They wanted Yildiz back. This is what happened next.

> Taj-ud-din raised troops with great secrecy and expedition, advanced towards Ghazni, and surprised Qutub-ud-din,

---

[10] Briggs, *History of the Rise of the Mahomedan Power in India till the Year A.D. 1612*, Vol. 1, 199.

who had no intelligence of his design till the day before his arrival. It was now too late to attempt a defence, so he was compelled to abandon Ghazni and retire to Lahore.[11]

Yildiz had extracted his sweet revenge. But Aibak had learnt two valuable lessons. The first was the realisation that the brutal, unscrupulous and violently restless politics of Central Asia was not for him. The second was waking up to the fact that he still controlled substantial chunks of territories in mainland Hindustan. Accordingly, he remained in Lahore for the paltry remainder of his life, fiercely policing it against Yildiz's designs on Hindustan. The move paid handsome dividends. By deliberately sundering all ties with Ghazni, Qutub-ud-din Aibak had near-permanently disconnected[12] Ghazni's overlordship of northern India. By the time of his death, this had evolved into a precedent of a foreign policy of sorts. However, it was still largely an unfinished business.

But his intense involvement in the politics of northwestern India and Central Asia meant that he rapidly lost vast expanses of the territories that Muhammad of Ghori had conquered with his able support. When he took over the reins of power in 1206, the Rajputs had already wrested the Chandela capital, Kalinjara[13], from Muslim clutches. Harishchandra, the king of the Gahadawalas, had snatched Badaun and Farrukhabad, and the doughty Pratiharas had regained Gwalior. Qutub-ud-din neither had the time nor the energy to punish them or to make fresh conquests in mainland India. It was a blot on his brilliant and highly successful military career so far: a reckless squandering of Muhammad of Ghori's tenacious conquests, which he had credulously handed over to his trusted slave Aibak.

---
[11] Ibid.
[12] For a good discussion on Aibak, see Srivastava, *The Sultanate of Delhi*, 88–92.
[13] Modern-day Bundelkhand.

Little Finger

'Little Finger' Qutub-ud-din Aibak was born of humble origins in remote Turkistan to Turkic parents. As a boy, he was bought by a slave merchant and sold to a *qazi* named Fakhr-ud-din at Nishapur.[14] The *qazi* took pity on him and educated him along with his sons in reading the Quran, horse riding and archery. When the *qazi* died an untimely death, his sons sold Aibak to a wealthy merchant who in turn sold him to Muhammad of Ghori in the city of Ghazni. Aibak, literally meaning 'little finger'[15], quickly earned Muhammad's favour and climbed up the ranks by dint of sheer humility and unquestioned obedience. But it was due to his solid performance in the decisive Second Battle of Tarain in 1192 that he attained the status of military *supremo* in Muhammad's army. The sultan awarded him the title of Qutub-ud-din, 'the Pole Star of the Faithful'. More goodies followed in its wake. Muhammad entrusted *all* his future conquests in Hindustan to Qutub-ud-din Aibak. He now had absolute freedom and power to take any decision regarding Hindustan.

Qutub-ud-din didn't disappoint. He established a temporary base at Indraprastha near Delhi. Then he occupied Delhi itself by forcibly ejecting a Chahamana feudatory in early 1193. Meanwhile, Hariraja, the brother of the late Prithviraja Chahamana, revolted at Ajmer and recaptured it. It was the fulfilment of a collective seething passion to avenge the death of the beloved Prithviraja Chahamana who had fallen not to valour but foul betrayal. However, when Qutub-ud-din marched with a massive force, Hariraja and his army withdrew. Meanwhile in Delhi, the ejected

---

[14] Now in the Khorasan Razavi Province, Iran.
[15] The meaning of the word is disputed. According to some scholars, Aibak might also mean the name of a tribe or a town.

Chahamana feudatory spotted his chance and reoccupied his former domain. Qutub-ud-din rushed back and laid a siege. It was time to teach a permanent lesson to these stubborn infidels. However, Hariraja was again free to recoup his strength. The Chahamana's force in Delhi, confident in their superior numbers, charged out with bravado to meet Qutub-ud-din's siege head-on. It was a particularly gruesome and bloody battle. The massacre on both sides was so extraordinary that the 'river Jamuna was discoloured with blood.' In the end, the Hindu force lost and retreated into the walls of the garrison and eventually surrendered after a prolonged siege. Hasan Nizami celebrates the victory in glowing turns of phrase.

> The Rai [Raja] who had fled from Delhi had raised an army of idolatrous ... tribes, the vapour of pride and conquest having entered his thoughtless brain. Qutub-ud-din pursued him, and when the wretch was taken, his head was severed from his body...[16]

Delhi irretrievably fell to the alien Turkic invader, an episode that marks a historical presage. Qutub-ud-din made it his capital, the first capital of what would eventually be called the alien Muslim Sultanate in India.

Qutub-ud-din then marched towards Kol (modern Aligarh)[17] after crossing the Jamuna, whose exceedingly pure waters 'resembled a mirror'. For the longest time, Kol

---

[16] Hasan Nizami, "Taju-l Ma'asir," 220.
[17] Also known as Koil before the 18th century. Its origins are obscure. A Puranic account narrates that Balarama slew the demon named Kol in this region and with the help of the Ahir people, established peace and order. Another account attributes the establishment of this city to the Dor Rajputs in the 4th century. The latter account can reasonably be verified by the ruins of the Dor Fort still standing in Aligarh. For fuller details, see Edwin T. Atkinson, *Descriptive and Historical Account of the Aligarh District* (Allahabad: North Western Frontier Provinces Government Press, 1875), 348.

had earned fame as one of the 'most celebrated fortresses of Hind'. Its capture would be of strategic importance. Aibak assaulted the citadel repeatedly till it fell and the infidels inside it 'who were wise accepted the light of Islam' but those who 'stood by their ancient faith were slain with the sword'[18]. His chiefs and nobles burst inside and 'carried off much treasures and countless plunder', including one thousand horses.

The original destroyer of Varanasi

Then the news reached him there: his sultan, Muhammad of Ghori, had decided to return to Hindustan for a fresh wave of devastation, whose central purpose was to punish Raja Jayachandra, the king[19] of the Gahadawala dynasty ruling the Antaravedi country in the Kanauj region. Flourishing commercial centres and sacred pilgrimage spots, including Kanyakubja and Kashi, were under his control. Qutub-ud-din marched forthwith and received his master and had the honour of kissing his hands, an act considered to be the 'highest of glories'. After this, he submitted an elephant laden with gold, silver and rubies, a hundred horses and all kinds of perfumes. And then the sultan and his slave strategised and prepared for the upcoming expedition against the infidel Jayachandra. When the roll call was taken, it amounted to a whopping fifty-thousand-strong cavalry, a good chunk of it supplied by Qutub-ud-din. Indeed, Muhammad had wisely not underestimated the prowess and fighting force of Jayachandra. Aibak led the vanguard with a thousand-strong cavalry and met Jayachandra at Chandawar on the

---

[18] Nizami, "Taju-l Ma'asir," 222.
[19] Jayachandra is the same Jaichand mentioned in the epic poem *Prithviraj Raso* which blames him for betraying Prithviraja Chahamana. The account is historically inaccurate. However, the name Jaichand unfortunately continues to be synonymous with 'traitor'.

banks of the Yamuna in a vast plain between Etawah and Kanauj. It was an evenly matched contest with neither side relenting. At one point, Jayachandra gained the upper hand forcing the Muslim army to backtrack. Given the copious and confusing historical chronicles of this landmark Battle of Chandawar, the actual details are hazy. However, a common thread emerges with reasonable accuracy. Either Aibak himself or someone in his army fatally shot Jayachandra with an arrow. The Gahadawala king fell on the ground from his elephant. A familiar scene unfolded in the Hindu army. Instead of protecting their king and commander-in-chief by fighting with greater intensity, they gave in to confusion and chaos. Quite naturally, Qutub-ud-din turned it to his advantage. It was the most opportune moment to purge 'the impurities of idolatry' and rid 'the country of Hind from vice and superstition'. The words in quotes are perhaps the mildest selections from the descriptions given by the Muslim chroniclers of the wanton orgy of genocide and bloodletting of Hindus that followed. It makes for truly sickening reading. Bestiality was unleashed on an appalling scale—heartless, random massacre, pillage, plunder, destruction and rape were carried out as a grand celebration. Hindu temples and shrines and *murtis* were broken and burnt and razed to the ground and their accumulated treasures, offered as *naivedya* (offerings made to god) by countless devotees over centuries, were looted in one go. It was Somanatha all over again on a slightly smaller scale. Hasan Nizami and Firishta differ in their descriptions of this ghastly event only in detail and phraseology. Nizami exults at this 'distribution of justice' and 'repression of idolatry' while Firishta proudly narrates that 'the number of infidels slain on just this day' was so staggering that it was long 'before the body of' Jayachandra could be found by his friends who had been allowed to search the mountain of corpses.

Muhammad of Ghori was elated but still hungry.

The peerless ancient centre of *Sanatana* Dharma, the home of every *Sanatana* sect, path and school, the repose of all the thirty-three crore deities in the Hindu pantheon, the Maha-Smashana (the Great Graveyard that liberates one from the endless cycle of birth and death) guarded by Mahadeva, the kotwal himself ... was now left wholly defenceless. Kashi. Varanasi. Banares. The city that exuded the radiance of the highest, the deepest and the most profound yearnings of philosophy and spirituality. A radiance that was couched in the root of its very name: Kashi, from the Sanskrit root, *kash*, meaning light, effulgent. Now it was prey to the aforementioned 'distribution of justice', a pious act that involved the pitiless destruction of *one thousand temples* and the construction of an equal number of mosques on the same foundations using the debris of these razed temples. Varanasi's very first and fiendish brush with the faith of peace and light permanently altered and marred its physical landscape. Needless to say, the collective wealth of all these temples added to Muhammad's unquenchable thirst to plunder this infidel land.

Next, he proceeded unimpeded to the Gahadawala Fort at Asni[20] where Jayachandra's treasury was located and pillaged it completely. An estimate of the staggering booty that Muhammad obtained during just this expedition is given by (1) Firishta: four thousand camels were loaded with the said spoils and (2) Ibn Asir: fourteen hundred camels loaded with plunder. Before Muhammad finally departed for Ghazni, 'the record of his celebrated holy wars had been

---

[20] The precise location of Asni is unclear. Some scholars identify it as the Asni village in the Fatehpur district, Uttar Pradesh. For example, see D.P. Dubey, 'A Note on the Identification of Asni', *Bulletin of the Deccan College Research Institute 68/69* (2008): 231–236.

written in histories and circulated throughout the breadth of Hindustan.

The fateful Battle of Chandawar was as pivotal and history-altering as the Second Battle of Tarain. The latter battle had not only blasted the gates of northern India wide open but also left its real impact on the psyche of the powerful Hindu rulers who perhaps for the first time felt vulnerable. However, with the death of Jayachandra and the collapse of the Gahadawala Empire, a significant swathe of north and eastern India faced the same prospect. The holiest of holy centres of *Sanatana* Dharma, Varanasi itself had been sacked so brutally.

Around the same period—by the late 12th century, a semi-barbaric Turkic adventurer named Ikhtiyar-ud-din Muhammad Bakhtiyar Khalji who had accompanied Muhammad of Ghori from Ghazni set up his independent freelance shop in Hindustan. Reckless, ruthless, brutal and daring, he quickly assembled a bunch of like-minded, barbarian freebooters and blazed a campaign of genocide and plunder across the Karmanasa River in the Magadha territory and soon razed the university towns of Odantapuri and Vikramashila and scorched the fabled Nalanda university. The grim and tragic story of the destruction of Nalanda, which burnt continuously for six long months, is too well known to repeat here. To his astonishment, he found thousands of 'shaven-headed Brahmans' (Buddhist monks) as sitting ducks. They didn't even bother to resist him as he massacred them with glee. The few who survived fled as far as Tibet. With the same lightning speed, he stormed into Navadwipa (modern-day Nadia, birthplace of Chaitanya Mahaprabhu) and snatched it from the Sena ruler, Lakshmanasena. Technically, Bhaktiyar Khalji was a feudatory of, and paid tribute to, Qutub-ud-din Aibak.

And so, by the time Muhammad of Ghori left for Ghazni after devastating Varanasi, the Ghurid Empire in India resembled a large arched bow that encompassed Arbudaranya (Mount Abu) on one end and Kalinjara (Bundelkhand) on the other. There would no longer exist even a *possibility* of the emergence of a unified Hindu Empire in the entire northern India, an overarching term that includes Bihar, Bengal, Uttar Pradesh, Madhya Pradesh and, to an extent, Gujarat.

The lost Aryavarta Consciousness had culminated[21] in a self-inflicted Hindu political explosion whose scattered fragments would never come together again.

Fresh troubles had erupted elsewhere for Qutub-ud-din Aibak, leaving him no time to leisurely savour the pious victory and his share of the lavish plunder seized at Varanasi and Asni. The Hindu rulers had merely accepted a military defeat but had not given up. The abhorrent outrages that followed in the wake of each Muslim invasion and attack had etched a permanent hatred in their minds for these despicable Turushkas. Big or small, whenever they found an opening, a weakness, they hit back. Now, it was with Kol and Ajmer. In 1195, just a year later, the Dor[22] Rajputs laid siege to wrest back this famous garrison now under Muslim control. However, the brave endeavour

---

[21] For a brilliant and insightful analysis of the collapse of Hindu kingdoms in northern India, see Majumdar, "Causes of the Collapse of Hindu Rule," in *The History and Culture of the Indian People*, Vol. 5, p. 125–129.
[22] Also spelt Dhor.

failed miserably, brutally. The Dor Rajputs were akin[23] to foxes 'playing with lions', who were swiftly dispatched to the 'fire of hell'. Three bastions were raised 'as high as heaven' with the severed heads of these Rajputs signalling a grave warning. Their carcasses 'became the food of beasts of prey'. And then, as was customary, the entire land was 'freed from idols and idol worship, and the foundations of infidelity were destroyed'. Ajmer proved tougher. The unsubdued brother of Prithviraja Chahamana, the same Hariraja had not only recouped his strength but had also made some smart alliances to harass Aibak. One such alliance was with a Jat chieftain who was marching against Aibak's Delhi stronghold itself. A measure of the kind of fear his march induced is given by Hasan Nizami in his typical style:

> The Jat supported by an army hastened to the borders of Delhi, and the people were suddenly caught in the darkness of his oppression and turbulence, and the blood and property of the Musulmans fell into danger and destruction.[24]

Meanwhile, Hariraja had invested the massive fort of Ajmer that originally, rightfully belonged to his deceased brother; Ajmer was indeed the proud inheritance of the Chahamanas, and every effort to recover it counted. This *third* rebellion in a space of two years against Muslim occupation was a courageous act of reclamation but in Nizami's eyes, it was a 'standard of perdition ... fanned by the flames of idolatry in his heart' and therefore had 'delivered the reins of vanity into the hands of Satan, and having conceived the ladders of grandeur in his brain, had become proud'.[25] An incensed Qutub-ud-din left a military detachment to guard Delhi,

---

[23] Nizami, "Taju-l Ma'asir," 224.
[24] Ibid., 225.
[25] Ibid.

sped towards Ajmer and blocked the Jat chieftain who gave him a spirited battle but had to retreat all the way back into the fort of Ajmer. Aibak blockaded the fort, locking Hariraja within. The prolonged siege obtained the desired results: finding himself vastly outnumbered and having no escape route, Hariraja voluntarily embraced death by burning himself on the funeral pyre instead of facing the humiliation of surrender and inevitable captivity. Aibak barged into one of the most 'celebrated forts in Hind' and cut off infidelity and 'utterly' ripped out the foundations of idol worship. Nizami praises Qutub-ud-din as 'The Blessed Lamp' and gloats how the celebrated rajas and Ranas rubbed their foreheads on the ground before this lamp. Aibak annexed Ajmer to the Delhi dominions and left behind a Muslim governor.

When he returned to Delhi, he decided to commemorate this great victory by building the first-ever mosque in the city. But it was not enough to simply build the Quwwat-ul-Islam, the 'glory of Islam'. It necessitated an emphatic spectacle of what this glory meant in actual practice. Accordingly, he demolished[26] twenty-seven Hindu and Jain temples and used their debris as construction material. The Quwwat-ul-Islam is noted[27] for the Qutub Minar, the 'tower of victory', celebrating and stamping the first-ever Muslim conquest in the heart of Delhi. The same applies to the 'construction' of the Adhai Din Ka Jhonpra[28] mosque in

---

[26] 'The conqueror entered the city and its vicinity was freed from idols and idol-worship; and in the sanctuaries of the images of the gods, mosques were razed by the worshippers of the one God'— Nizami, quoted in Archeological Survey of India, *Qutab Minar & Adjoining Monuments* (Delhi: The Director General Archeological Survey of India, 2002), 31.

[27] The construction of the first storey of the Qutub Minar began some time in 1199.

[28] Literally, 'shed of two-and-half days'. Also known as Dhai Din ki Masjid. It was the second mosque to be built in India by the Mamluk slave kings, the first being the Quwwat-ul-Islam mosque in Delhi. For a detailed history of this mosque, see K.D.L. Khan, 'Ajmer's Adhai din ka Jhonpra', *The Tribune*, 2 September 2007.

Ajmer, built after razing down the existing Sanskrit College, which had housed a beautiful Saraswati temple within.

In 1195, Muhammad of Ghori returned to Hindustan. He was hungry again. Aided by Aibak, he quickly demolished the tiny principalities of Bayana and Gwalior, forcing their rulers into submission. They were strategic bastions but were also the centres of 'idolatry and perdition'. Both were annexed to the Delhi dominions. In late 1195 or early 1196, Muhammad returned to Ghazni.

The Mher Offensive

Which was when Qutub-ud-din Aibak was faced with a mortal threat to his own life. By a small band of courageous Hindu fighters. The indomitable Mhers at Ajmer. A valiant reminder and replay of the episode involving the hardy pastoral Jats who solidly thumped the invading Arab forces more than five hundred years ago. Both Prithviraja Chahamana and his proud brother Hariraja had died heroic deaths but the inspirational courage they had infused was still coursing throughout the land. The ever-vigilant Mhers were watchful, waiting for a moment of weakness on the part of the Turushka governor installed at Ajmer. They finally saw their chance. The Muslim force at Ajmer was indeed small and could be easily overcome with slight additional help. The Mhers sent their spies to the Chalukya King at Gujarat, Bhima II, with this request, plus an elaborate plan and strategy to mount a surprise night attack on the Turushkas and to also block their escape routes. The Mhers had done their homework painstakingly. Besides, it was their own ancestral land whose every nook and cranny they knew intimately. Bhima II readily agreed. But

Qutub-ud-din had received intelligence of this development and pre-empted the Mhers by launching an early morning offensive. However, the thoroughly prepared Mhers offered such a solid resistance that the battle lasted throughout the day, spilling over to the next morning. Which was when Bhima's massive army came to their assistance all the way from Anhilwara. The Muslim army was massacred on a large scale, and its commander who was grievously wounded retreated inside the fort. The Mhers didn't relent. After a dogged pursuit, they surrounded it and encamped within one *parasang* (about 3.5 miles) of it. Qutub-ud-din Aibak was thoroughly hemmed in. Panic set in. He quickly sent a message to his lord and master at Ghazni for reinforcements, which arrived in time. At this, the Mhers tactically withdrew.

However, Qutub-ud-din Aibak never forgot the humiliation. He spent the entire year shoring up his strength and mustering a powerful army. In 1196, he marched towards Anahilapataka. When Bhima II received the news, he opted for a non-confrontational approach and became untraceable. Aibak reached the solid fortresses of Pali and Nandul[29] and to his surprise, found them abandoned. Bhima II had made some shrewd calculations. He had entrusted the battle to the Vaghela vassal, Karna Deva,[30] and Dharavarsha Paramara[31]. Their combined forces were equal to if not greater than that of Aibak. And they had chosen their field of battle well. At the foothills of Mount Abu, the same location where the great sultan Muhammad of Ghori had his first taste of humiliating defeat at the hands of a mere boy. The psychological ploy worked. In Nizami's words, the 'Musulmans considered the location as a bad omen.' Aibak's

---

[29] It is difficult to locate these forts precisely but they lay in the general region between Ajmer and Mount Abu.
[30] Muslim chroniclers call him Rai Karan.
[31] Darabara, in Muslim chronicles.

massive force dithered. Which is when foolish bravado overcame the Hindu army. Assuming a foregone victory, they abandoned their positions at the strategic hill passes and surged out into the open field, baying for blood. At night, the Muslim army occupied these abandoned passes and when the open-field battle began, the Hindu army suffered heavy reverses. This was the final outcome:

> A severe action ensued from dawn to mid-day, when the army of idolatry and damnation turned its back in flight from the line of battle. Most of their leaders were taken prisoners, and nearly fifty thousand infidels were despatched to hell by the sword, and from the heaps of the slain, the hills and the plains became of one level…. More than twenty thousand slaves, and twenty elephants, and cattle and arms beyond all calculation, fell into the hands of the victors…. You would have thought that the treasures of the kings of all the inhabited world had come into their possession.[32]

Karna Deva managed to escape even as Aibak marched towards Anahilapataka. The same ghastly horror was repeated: Hindu and Jain temples were mercilessly demolished, *murtis* were smashed to pieces, homes were set ablaze, palaces and grand mansions were plundered with impunity and large-scale slave-taking ensued. Before leaving for Delhi, Aibak stationed a Muslim officer to take charge of this cindered excuse of a once-grand city. But no sooner had Aibak left, Bhima II emerged from his hiding place and drove out the Turushka officer and, over time, ejected most of the Turks from Gujarat. For the next full century, no Muslim king from Delhi dared venture into Gujarat.

---

[32] Nizami, "Taju-l Ma'asir," 230.

Another wave of rebellions arose, a chronic theme that marked and stood out like an eyesore throughout Qutub-ud-din's career as a military general and as the founder of the Delhi Sultanate in India. The stupendous victory attained at the Battle of Chandawar proved short-lived. He had to recapture Kanauj, Badaun and their surrounding regions. The same held true for large parts of Rajputana. After he recaptured Nadol, the Chahamanas fled from there but didn't give up. They founded new branches and extended their bloodlines at Kotah, Bundi and Sirohi. But the rebellion at Kalinjara and Mahoba proved a terrible headache. The intrepid Chandelas had risen their head again under Raja Paramardi or Paramal who harassed Aibak continuously. In the final battle in 1202, he retreated into the mighty Kalinjara Fort after a spirited resistance. However, he yielded once Aibak completely cut off the fort from the outside world and offered to pay tribute. But he died before he could do that. In a courageous act of defiance, his stubborn minister Ajaya Deva repudiated the agreement and fought back with everything he had. But drought played spoilsport and he was compelled to abandon the fort. Qutub-ud-din annexed all of Kalinjara, Mahoba and Khajuraho and installed a Turkish general there, but not before completing a pious task, which Nizami praises with such warm piety.

> The temples were converted into mosques and abodes of goodness, and the ejaculations of the bead-counters and the voices of the summoners to prayer ascended to the highest heaven, and the very name of idolatry was annihilated.... Fifty thousand men came under the collar of slavery, and the land became black as pitch with Hindus.[33]

---

[33] Ibid., 232.

Death by polo

All of these impressive, extensive conquests made over a lifetime had again passed into infidel hands. Qutub-ud-din Aibak had achieved them all in service of his master and sultan, Mu'izz ad-Din Muhammad Ghori. And now, when he himself was sultan, most of them had slipped away. Large parts of Rajputana were gone. With the death of the 'Splendour of Islam', Bakhtiyar Khalji, parts of Bengal and Bihar were in turmoil and openly defied the authority of Delhi. Bundelkhand was gone. Kanauj was gone. Gwalior had fallen to the Pratihara idolater. This then was the *third* bitter lesson that he had learnt, the outcome of his wistful contemplation in his palace at Lahore about his shameful ouster from Ghazni at the hands of the wretch Yildiz. At this late stage in his life, Qutub-ud-din Aibak decided that the wise course was to consolidate what remained of Muhammad of Ghori's conquests in India, a precedent his successors followed for roughly a century. He was no longer in a position to make any fresh conquests in Hindustan in his new status as sultan and reconciled himself to it. Like all Muslim sultans, Qutub-ud-din Aibak was deeply bigoted and exceedingly cruel. His destruction of Hindu and Jain temples runs in thousands and his barbaric genocide of the infidels into lakhs. He did not distinguish himself in any other manner unless one counts the building of the Quwwat-ul-Islam mosque after demolishing temples as a distinction.

Qutub-ud-din Aibak was not destined to rule for long. An addict of the *chowgan* game (polo), he fell from his horse[34] in a freak accident, fatally damaged his ribs and died in 1210. He was buried in Lahore, an episode his

---

[34] The polo ground was called *Bagh-e-Chowgan*.

flatterer-cum-hagiographer Hasan Nizami says was akin to burying a 'treasure in the bowels of the earth'.

While Qutub-ud-din Aibak deserves credit for sundering all ties with Ghazni and thereby preventing further, destructive Muslim raids from Central Asia, he also heralded a new power structure and centre that would endure for the next six hundred years. For the first time in the long history of ancient Bharatavarsha, Delhi became the seat of a prolonged, oppressive religious despotism concentrating all power within itself. So far, the city, at various points, had at best been a principality, governorship and protectorate. With due regard to vastly changed historical and political circumstances, it can reasonably be said that a basic element in the template that Qutub-ud-din Aibak had set has continued till date, minus the religious despotism: Delhi continues to be the political centre of modern India, shorn of any traces of the native classical culture and civilisation.

The three separate Mamluk[35] Turkic slave dynasties that followed Aibak made no new conquests in India during their regimes but shored up control over the existing ones. What all three faced throughout their rule was what Aibak had also faced but could never overcome: incessant uprisings from various Hindu kingdoms, large and tiny, who never accepted this alien Turkish rule and kept strengthening their

---

[35] 'Mamluk' literally means 'owned', from the Arabic word, *malak*: to possess. It is based on the Quranic term for a slave, 'and what your right hands possess'. For valuable discussions on the applicability of the term 'slave dynasties' to the first three sultans of Delhi, see: (1) Srivastava, *The Sultanate of Delhi*, 88–9; (2) Majumdar, *The History and Culture of the Indian People*, Vol. 5, 159 (3) Jackson, *The Delhi Sultanate: A Political and Military History*, 44. The term 'slave dynasty' used in this book is in the limited sense of the origins of Qutub-ud-din Aibak, Iltutmish and Balban as Turkic slaves who were brought to India by their masters.

forces and kept their attempts alive to wrest back their lost lands in the hope that their ancient Dharma would flourish once again.

Slave of a slave

Because Aibak died before he could formally appoint a successor, a factional battle broke out, characteristic of all such battles in the Muslim scheme of political succession. At Lahore, Qutub-ud-din's son Aram Shah wasted no time in declaring himself the legitimate sultan propped up[36] by the Sirjandar Turki, 'who was the leader of all sedition', the bloodthirsty Turk 'who had opened his hand to spill the blood of Musulmans'. What both Aram Shah and his instigator the Sirjandar hadn't realised was that the real power centre had already made an imperceptible shift to Delhi. The loyalists of Aibak, the powerful nobility of the *amirs* detested this weakling son of their late sultan. Led by Ali-i-Ismail, the *amir-i-dad* (chief magistrate), this faction extended an invitation to the *muqti* (governor) of Badaun to take over the throne at Delhi. The *muqti* was Qutub-ud-din's trusted slave and son-in-law, Shams-ud-din Iltutmish, who gladly accepted the offer in 1211. Although Aram Shah managed to raise a 'fine army' and marched towards Iltutmish after about eight months, his so-called retaliation ended[37] in obvious disaster. While Hasan Nizami, the wily author of *Taju-l Ma'asir* doesn't even take Aram Shah's name, he nevertheless gloats about the ghastly fate of Sirjandar Turki in lines laden with violence.

> Turki threw himself into the waters of the Jamuna, took to flight like a fox in fear of a lion, and departed by the way

---

[36] Nizami, "Taju-l Ma'asir," 237.
[37] For a discussion about the end of Aram Shah, see Jackson, *The Delhi Sultanate: A Political and Military History*, 29.

of river and hill like a crocodile and a leopard, and, starting and trembling, concealed himself in the jungles and forests, like a sword in a scabbard, or a pen in a writing-box.[38]

In the same eight months, Aram Shah's inheritance, the first-ever Muslim sultanate in Hindustan, had imploded chaotically. Aibak's slave-compatriot under Muhammad of Ghori, the ambitious Nasir-ud-din Qubachah easily occupied Multan and Bhatinda and nibbled parts of Lahore itself. As long as Aibak was alive, Qubachah remained content as the governor of Uch. Likewise, Ali Mardan Khalji, the governor of Bengal, declared independence. Iltutmish had Delhi under his control. In the somewhat compassionate words of Firishta, Aram Shah was 'ill adapted to govern such an empire'.

Iltutmish was a slave of a slave. He originally hailed from a noble Ilbari Turkish family from Central Asia but his own brothers, jealous of his intelligence and ability, forcibly sold him as a slave in early boyhood. A merchant named Jamal-ud-din bought him and took him to Ghazni and from there to Delhi. Qutub-ud-din Aibak bought him for fifty thousand pieces of silver the moment he set his eyes on this handsome boy. He groomed him diligently, promoted him rapidly and even gave his daughter in marriage.

Yet, when Iltutmish sat on the throne of Delhi, his position was exceedingly vulnerable. The fledgling sultanate that Aibak had carved in Hindustan had already shattered

---

[38] Nizami, "Taju-l Ma'asir," 237. See also, Nizami, in *Qutab Minar & Adjoining Monuments*, 31.

into four pieces in less than a year. Worse trouble ensued. Aibak's other powerful adversary, the accursed Taj-ud-din Yildiz who had kicked him out of Ghazni had now become aggressive again. Yildiz sent the word: *he* was the sovereign of Hindustan and Iltutmish, his vassal. Iltutmish readily agreed and accepted the insignia befitting a vassal: the canopy (*chhatra*) and the mace (*durbash*). The successor of Aibak had wisely not declared himself the sultan but merely a king. Iltutmish's time would come—four or five years later. Yildiz's imperial pretensions as the sovereign of Hindustan were violently smashed in 1215–1216 by the marauding Khwarezmian Shah who tossed him out of Ghazni. Humiliated and furious, Yildiz stormed into Lahore and expelled Qubachah. Then he put forward a haughty demand harbouring the delusion that Iltutmish had honestly accepted his vassalage: 'send me your troops so I can reoccupy Ghazni.' It appears that Nizami, the flatterer, was more incensed at this than Iltutmish himself.

> [M]essengers arrived frequently from Taj-ud din, who had admitted into his brain the wind of pride and the arrogance of dominion...[39]

Yildiz had grossly underestimated Iltutmish's patience to swallow a temporary insult and had overlooked the kind of strength that he had built up in these five years. It was time to teach Yildiz a lesson one final time. On 25 January 1216, the historic battleground of Tarain once again became the theatre for another decisive encounter: this time, not between invader and infidel but invader and invader. While Firishta's account of the battle is largely restrained, Hasan Nizami becomes unhinged regurgitating his pet analogy

---

[39] Nizami, "Taju-l Ma'asir," 239.

of fox-and-lion, chess terminology and forces of nature, all of which favoured Iltutmish. Ultimately, Yildiz suffered a grievous arrow wound, was captured, imprisoned and, according to some accounts, poisoned to death in jail at Badaun. With the death of Yildiz, Iltutmish had finally completed the work that Aibak had begun: Delhi was now completely out of the reach of Ghazni.

A detour of history

Perhaps the history of India would've permanently been altered even as Iltutmish was gradually consolidating his power but for a crucial detour.

In 1218, Temujin Borjigin, or Genghis Khan, swept down from the Tartary steppes at the head of a smothering tidal wave of a monster troop numbering over a lakh. This was one of his largest-ever expeditions, whose sole purpose was to annihilate the pompous Khwarezmian Shah, Ala-ad-din Muhammad II, together with his vast empire: the same Ala-ad-din Muhammad who had chucked out Yildiz from Ghazni. Needless to mention, Ala-ad-din didn't stand a chance against the Mongols and decamped to an unknown island on the Caspian coast and died there three heartbroken years later. His equally terrified son, Jalal-ad-din Mangbarni[40] darted through Khurasan and Afghanistan and finally sought refuge in Punjab, doggedly pursued by the terrible Mongols who had by then devastated almost ninety per cent of the Khwarezmian Empire in Persia. Mangbarni, the fugitive, and not the invader, met with impressive success in Punjab when he initially stationed himself in the Sindh Sagar Doab. Then, he sealed an alliance with a powerful Khokhar chief by marrying his daughter. His Mongol pursuers were advised by Genghis

---
[40] Also spelled Mingbarni.

Khan to stand guard on the other side of the Sindhu River and extract him at any cost. Now, Mangbarni the fugitive transformed himself into an aggressor. One of the first things he did was to disgorge Qubachah from Lahore. Then he nibbled away large portions of the Ravi and Chenab regions, wrested Sialkot and moved down towards Lahore. After that, he sent an envoy to Iltutmish: 'give me asylum; join hands with me, we'll crush the Mongols'. Iltutmish was confronted perhaps with the greatest-ever threat to his newfound autonomy, survival itself. He didn't wish to anger the Mongols lurking just across the Sindhu River by allying with this fugitive-turned-invader. Worse still, he didn't want to invite an avoidable threat by allowing Mangbarni to remain so close to Delhi. The perilous situation taxed his diplomatic skills to the fullest. Iltutmish gambled. He had the envoy murdered in secret and sent Mangbarni a dodgy reply. To which a furious Mangbarni prepared to march against him but for some reason, abandoned the plan. At any rate, he seems to have realised that it was untenable to stay in India any longer. But before exiting the country via Kirman, he embarked on a frenzied spate of devastation, setting fire to Uch, sacking and plundering Siwan and forcing out the ruler of Debal. Iltutmish quickly moved to fill the vacuum. He reoccupied Lahore and then easily expelled the thoroughly weakened Qubachah from Multan. The latter fled to the island fortress at Bhakkar[41] only to find himself trapped from all directions. Unwilling to be taken prisoner, he jumped into the Sindhu River and drowned to death on the night of 26 May 1228. Meanwhile, the military officers of Iltutmish had brought more good news: both Uch and Debal had fallen and acknowledged the supremacy of Delhi.

---

[41] Now in Pakistan.

It was the ultimate victory for Iltutmish. He had successfully staved off the terrible Mongols *and* upheld Aibak's 'no Central Asian politics' foreign policy.

Two interesting religio-historical perspectives emerge from Iltutmish's deft handling of the Genghis Khan episode. The *first* is the absolute silence of Iltutmish's hagiographer-cum-historian Minhaju-s Siraj on his patron's refusal to support Mangbarni, a fellow Musulman against the infidel Mongols (who were Shamanists). Siraj's entire account of Iltutmish drips with honeyed flattery: 'great and religious king', 'invincible king', 'Delhi was adorned by his presence,' 'chosen by the destiny of Providence'. Likewise, Ibn-al-Athir, also known as Ibn Asir, author of *Kamil-ut-Tawarikh*, mentions nothing about this incident. Firishta altogether dismisses it as if nothing had occurred. This is entirely in keeping with the mindset and approach[42] of the typical medieval Muslim chronicler: the sultan could do no wrong because he was the champion who spread the light of Islam in infidel lands. And in the event that he committed acts construed as going against the tenets of the Only True Faith, silence, evasion or whitewashing or all three was the best recourse. Thus, Iltutmish's case—like scores of other sultans—is quite representative of the hollowness of the unity and infallibility of the global (or 'universal') Muslim ummah. Iltutmish's anxiety to preserve his own nascent imperialism trumped his fidelity towards Islam. The *second* is the aforementioned detour taken by history. But for it, the

---

[42] For insightful discussions on the attitude, approach and historiography of medieval Muslim chroniclers, see: (1) Smith, *The Oxford History of India*, xx–xxi, 223 (2) Peter Hardy, *Historians of Medieval India* (London: Luzac & Company, 1966) (3) Jackson, *The Delhi Sultanate: A Political and Military History*, 32–3, and more fully, "Chapter 3: Sultans and Sources." (4) Lal, "Chapter 2: Historiography of Medieval India," in *The Legacy of Muslim Rule in India*.

following outcome would have likely occurred, according to the historical scholar A.L. Srivastava.

> Changiz Khan, who was probably not desirous of violating a neutral state, returned from Afghanistan. Delhi was thus saved. *Had he chosen a different course, the Sultanate of Delhi would have been finished in its infancy* [emphasis added]. But the country, in all likelihood, would have gained, for *the Mongols, unlike the Turks, would gradually have merged in Hindu society as they were Shamanists and had much in common with the Indian people* [emphasis added].[43]

Although Iltutmish had managed to decisively consolidate the four different but chaotic divisions of the infant sultanate in the northwest, he had suffered extraordinary reverses elsewhere in Hindustan, chiefly in Rajputana. A sixteen-year-long neglect[44] of this extensive part of his dominion was a long time. The Hindus had mercilessly evicted the hated Turushka governors in these regions. The indefatigable Govindaraja Chauhan at Ranthambhor had chased out the Turkish troops and imposed his sovereignty on Jodhpur and its surroundings. The same had occurred in the Muslim dominions at Jalor, Nadol, Mandor, Barmer, Ratnapur, Sanchor, Radhadhara, Khera, Ramasin, Bhinamal, Alwar, Bayana, Thangir and Ajmer. And right across the Ranthambhor border, the Pratiharas hailing from the Kachchhapaghata dynasty had dismantled the Muslim garrison at Gwalior. Further down, southeast of Gwalior, the

---

[43] Srivastava, *The Sultanate of Delhi*, 97.
[44] A point that Peter Jackson observes: 'We cannot fail to be struck, again, by the relative absence of campaigns against the Hindu powers. During the first sixteen years of his reign, Iltutmish is known to have conducted only one such expedition, against the Chawhan ruler of Jalor ... [the campaign] is undated.'—*The Delhi Sultanate: A Political and Military History*, 30.

solid fortress of Kalinjara and Ajaigarh had been pocketed back into the Chandela fold.

Beginning his campaigns of revanche in 1226, Iltutmish wrested Ranthambhor, Mandor, Jalor and other regions, but all of them came at a huge cost, and he was compelled to allow these infidel kings to rule as his vassals. An absolute Muslim rule was impossible. Besides, he suffered two additional humiliations. At Nagada, in the heartland of the Guhilots, he had to endure a crushing defeat at the hands of its king, Kshetra Singh. This was followed by another severe drubbing at Gujarat where the Chalukya king browbeat him to retreat. Similarly, his forays into Bundelkhand and Malwa proved largely ineffective. Even worse, Iltutmish's commander, Malik Tayasai, while returning from Bundelkhand, was waylaid and severely pounded by Chahadadeva[45] of the Yajvapala[46] dynasty, which was in the ascendant. The Muslim sultans of Delhi couldn't touch the Paramaras in Malwa for the remainder of the century. Iltutmish's reconquest attempts further eastwards from Kalinjara, in the Ganga–Jamuna Doab, resulted in unmemorable successes. The infidels simply wouldn't stop fighting back. Important centres like Badaun, Kanauj, Varanasi, Katehar[47], Bahraich and Awadh had to be made to resubmit to Delhi with extraordinary difficulty. But Awadh wouldn't submit so easily. No sooner had Iltutmish left, a doughty leader of a local tribe, Prithu (or Bartu) mounted a vicious fightback, sending shockwaves in the Muslim camp. Iltutmish had left behind his son Nasir-ud-din Mahmud as the governor of Awadh. Bartu's sudden, daring

---

[45] Titled Rana Chahir Ajari.
[46] Jajapella or Jajpella dynasty who ruled from Narwar, Madhya Pradesh.
[47] Katehar's capital was Ahicchatra, one of the great centres of Hindu civilisation, culture and philosophy. It was the northern capital of the Panchala kingdom, so central to the story of the Mahabharata.

and repeated raids resulted in the extraordinary slaughter of Muslim soldiers. Minhaju-s Siraj angrily records how under Bartu's sword, more than one lakh twenty thousand Musulmans 'received martyrdom'. Likewise in Chandawar and Tirhut, constant rebellions, unanticipated insurrections and recurring disturbances proved a permanent headache for Iltutmish. Any victory attained[48] was in the nature of 'personal triumphs' which were 'short-lived and local in effect'. Perhaps, the only lasting success of Iltutmish's attempts at re-conquest was in Bengal. It was ruled by Husam-ud-Ewaz who had bestowed upon himself the title, sultan Ghiyas-ud-din Khalji and rejected the authority of Delhi. Iltutmish sent his son Nasir-ud-din to punish him. In 1228, Nasir-ud-din invaded Bengal, defeated and eventually killed Ewaz and plundered his treasury.

The decisive victory in Bengal added prestige, fear and respect for his rule both within and outside his kingdom. But Iltutmish knew that alone would not be sufficient to stamp his emergent authority as sultan. A more emphatic ingredient was needed to calcify it. A sagacious and cautious ruler, he was constantly awake to the fact that he was still a candidate nominated by the powerful Turkic nobles and chiefs who saw him merely as their peer seated on a slightly higher chair. Then, Iltutmish delivered his master stroke. Through skilful diplomacy, he managed to invite the envoy of the Abbasid Caliph, Al-Mustansir, to his court at Delhi in February 1229. At a lavish and elaborate banquet, the envoy presented Iltutmish robes of honour and a diploma from the Caliph, which conclusively stamped his suzerainty. Then he was also bestowed with grand titles, such as *Yamin Khalifat Allah* (Right Hand of God's Deputy), *Nasir Amir al-Muminin* (Commander of the Faithful) and *Khalifa-yi*

---

[48] Majumdar, *The History and Culture of the Indian People*, Vol. 5, 185.

Amir al-Mu'minin (Deputy of the Commander of the Faithful). In the caustic observation[49] of the historian and scholar Peter Jackson, this was an elaborate charade where the usurper Iltutmish had thus attained respectability as one of the family of orthodox Muslim princes whose rule enjoyed the highest possible sanction.

But the full, ridiculous extent of this charade becomes clearer when we examine the broader context. By the 13th century, the Caliphate itself was a heap of broken pieces of independent Muslim nations of various sizes. Yet, by a convenient political fiction, these new and independent Muslim States recognised the Khalifa, at least in theory, as be their political and religious head or suzerain.[50]

The train of this charade would only escalate in the coming years. The deadly Mongol-Buddhist conqueror Hulagu Khan stormed and ravaged Baghdad in 1258 and slaughtered the Caliph himself in a brutal[51] orgy of carnage. An uncle of the Caliph fled to Egypt as a refugee. In a bizarre twist of intrigue and religious piety, this uncle was recognised as the spiritual head of Islam, at least within Egypt.

'My Turkish slaves will preserve my name'

Iltutmish's act of astute diplomacy in seeking legitimacy from a transnational head[52] of a pretentious global religious imperialism stamped his authority like nothing else. He also became the only sultan from the Slave dynasties to

---

[49] Jackson, *The Delhi Sultanate: A Political and Military History*, 38.
[50] Srivastava, *The Sultanate of Delhi*, 130.
[51] According to most accounts of the period, the Caliph was rolled up inside a rug upon which the Mongols rode their horses. See for example, Ian Frazier, 'Annals of History: Invaders Destroying Baghdad', *The New Yorker*, 25 April 2005.
[52] Elliot and Dowson, *The History of India as Told by Its Own Historians*, Vol. 2, 294.

receive this formal but theoretical sovereign investiture from the Caliph. This gave him the absolute authority to mint coins in India in the Caliph's name. Iltutmish's first silver *tanka* weighed one hundred and seventy-five grains and had an Arabic inscription on it. With it, he became the first Turkic sultan to introduce purely Arabic coinage in India. Iltutmish also achieved another long-term outcome through this. He laid the foundation of a military–religious despotism, which reached its flagitious zenith under Ala-ud-din Khalji. This is his most notable legacy.

Like his predecessors, Iltutmish was also a pious Sunni Muslim and followed the dictates of his religion dutifully. He completed the construction of the Qutub Minar which Qutub-ud-din Aibak had commissioned. He never missed saying the five prayers daily and strictly observed all the prescribed Islamic rituals. He also harboured an inveterate hatred and intolerance towards the Shias and persecuted them on a significant scale, which led to an Ismaili Shia rebellion in Delhi whose declared goal was his assassination. Iltutmish suppressed it with shocking violence which resulted in their indiscriminate slaughter. Needless to mention, his policy towards Hindus was far worse. Towards the end of his life, around 1233–1234, he marched against the sacred city of Vidisha and razed its ancient Sun Temple. Next, he proceeded towards Ujjain, the beloved city of Kalidasa and of generations of poets, scholars and people of learning from the ancient times. It was the proudest and the pre-eminent centre of culture and commerce during the golden Gupta era. Ujjain was also home to the magnificent and sublime Mahakala Temple (or Mahakal) dedicated to Shiva, one of the twelve sacred Jyotirlingas. The immortal poet Kalidasa, an unparalleled devotee of Shiva, dedicates beautifully poignant verses[53] in his timeless poem *Meghaduta* to describe the Mahakala Temple complete with the evening Nada-Aradhana, the performance of music and dance before Shiva. Quite naturally, it was one of the great hubs of idolatry. With a savage stroke, Iltutmish demolished[54] this exquisite temple—a majestic, living proof and a profoundly dignified symbol of the possibilities of what innate devotion and stainless piety could accomplish when it finds unsullied expression in architecture and refined sculpture. A work of three hundred painstaking years and countless generations of dedicated, joyous, backbreaking work, an awe-inspiring system of transmitting generational knowledge, an economic framework and political stability that sustained all this tragically fell to the sword, pickaxe and the fire of a determined vandal. The Mahakala Temple is described by Firishta himself as

> magnificent ... surrounded by a wall one hundred cubits in height. The image of Vikramaditya, who had been formerly prince of this country, and so renowned, that the Hindus have taken an era[55] from his death, as also the image of Mahakal, both of stone, with many other figures of brass, were found in the temple.[56]

After the pious ravage was complete, Iltutmish ordered his troops to carry[57] these broken idols and 'many other figures' and 'brass statues of Vikramaditya and other notable rulers' to Delhi where they were 'broken at the door of the great'

---

[53] For example: In Chapter 1, or the *Purva Megha,* of the *Meghaduta,* Kalidasa launches on a vivid description of Ujjain, the beauty of the Shipra River and the grand Tandava dance performed in the evening.
[54] The temple was since rebuilt and is still renowned for its extraordinary *bhasmarti.*
[55] Vikramaditya Shaka.
[56] Briggs, *History of the Rise of the Mahomedan Power in India till the Year A.D. 1612,* Vol. 1, 211.
[57] Ibid.

Quwwat-ul-Islam mosque so that the Faithful could trample upon it.

———•·•·•———

There was another significant legacy Iltutmish had obliquely inherited from Muhammad of Ghori, who had famously declared before his death that

> Other monarchs may have one son, or two sons; I have thousands of sons, *my Turkish slaves who will be the heirs of my dominions, and who, after me, will take care to preserve my name in the Khuṭbah* [Friday sermon] *throughout these territories* [emphasis added].[58]

Accordingly, Iltutmish filled his court, administration, bureaucracy and army with immigrant[59] Turkic Muslim slaves and to a lesser extent with Ghuris and Tajiks. He had to largely thank Genghis Khan for this fortune. The Mongol's exhaustive devastation of the Khwarezmian Empire had all sorts of immigrants pouring into India, which they correctly assumed was a safe shelter. A good portion included men well versed in bureaucracy, law and war, while some were former nobles and high-ranking officers. This apart, like Muhammad of Ghori, Iltutmish also built a powerful corps of dedicated Turkic slaves (*bandagan*) known as Shamsis[60] who were loyal to his Royal Person alone[61]. Over time, these

---

[58] Minhaju-s Siraj, "Tabaqat-i-Nasiri," 294

[59] For a detailed exposition of this aspect, see Jackson, *The Delhi Sultanate: A Political and Military History*, 41–3.

[60] From whence the Shamsid dynasty gets its name.

[61] This was a rather common theme of Muslim despots across the medieval period. For instance, the 14th-century Ottoman sultan, Murat I, would regularly take slaves captured from various battles. Non-Muslim slaves would be converted to Islam, taught Turkish and inducted into this private army, known as 'the slaves of the Gate'. Their allegiance was only to the Sultan and not to his empire.

Turkic nobles would grow in power, exert direct influence on, and even dictate to, the sultan himself, earning the sobriquet of the Chahalgani, the dreaded 'forty'.

From this clique emerged the next sultan of Delhi: Baha' al-Din Balaban-i Khwurd ('the Lesser'), or simply, Balban.

The head of the dreaded Forty

Balban[62] was the last Ilbari Turk to rule the Delhi Sultanate after Iltutmish died in April 1236 due to a prolonged illness which he contracted en route to a botched attempt to invade Bamiyan.

Balban, whose father was a Khan of ten thousand families in Central Asia, was captured as a slave by the Mongols in his early youth. They sold him to a Sufi named Khwaja Jamal-ud-din at Ghazni, who nicknamed him Baha-ud-din and, in turn, sold him to Iltutmish at Delhi. Minhaju-s Siraj, whom Balban appointed as a *qazi* and awarded several important official positions, exhibits an exceptional degree of divine sycophancy when he traces his benefactor's origins.

> *The Almighty desired to grant support to the power of Islam and to the strength of the Muhammadan faith, to extend his glorious shadow over it, and to preserve Hindustan within the range of his favour.... He therefore removed Ulugh Khan [Balban] in his youth from Turkistan, and separated him from his race ... his tribe and relations, and conveyed him to the country (of Hindustan)* [emphasis added].... His success was so great that other nobles began to look upon it with jealousy, and the thorn of envy began to rankle in their hearts. *But it was the will of God that he should excel them all,* [emphasis added] so that the more the fire of their envy burnt, the stronger did the incense of his fortune rise from the censer

---

[62] His name is also pronounced as Balaban meaning, 'sparrow-hawk'. See Jackson, *The Delhi Sultanate: A Political and Military History*, 44.

of the times. They seek to extinguish the light of God with their mouths, but God willeth only to perfect his light.[63]

Notwithstanding Siraj's exalted eulogy, Balban was endowed with military competence, obsequious cunning, iron determination and the sort of predatory patience and precise timing that is required to capture the summit of unbridled political power. These qualities enabled him to bide his time through a labyrinthine concoction of strategies whose ultimate aim only he knew. And attained.

Because another legacy that Iltutmish had left behind was an official successor, unlike Aibak. In that sense, he was the first founder of the Slave dynasty of the Delhi Sultanate. The only able contender and potential successor to Iltutmish had been his eldest son, Nasir-ud-din Mahmud. However, the son had died before his father. As the military general who had defeated and killed the upstart Ewaz in Bengal, he had been rewarded with its governorship. However, Nasir-ud-din contracted some disease and died in 1229. In nominating his successor, Iltutmish set aside his inept and pleasure-loving second son, Rukn-ud-din Firoz, and publicly coronated his *daughter* Razia and minted a silver *tanka* to celebrate the occasion.

That was the beginning of a protracted, intra-family fracas for the throne which left behind a bloody trail of four regal bodies murdered, on an average, once every three years over the 1236–1246 decade. It also gave the Delhi Sultanate its first and last *sultana*. Even a brief sequence of these events makes for queasy reading. The throne of the Delhi Sultanate would not tolerate a woman, notwithstanding *sultan* Iltutmish's nomination. So, the debauched Rukn-ud-din Firoz was propped up by a powerful faction of nobles

---

[63] Minhaju-s Siraj, "Tabaqat-i-Nasiri," 360, 362. For the most part, Minhaju-s Siraj addresses and refers to Balban as Ulugh Khan.

in May 1236, which in turn was remote-controlled by the skilled intriguer, Shah Turkan, Rukn-ud-din's mother. In Firishta's words, 'this woman ... a Turki slave, was a monster of cruelty.' Almost immediately, she began to call the shots and went on an unbridled spree of vindictiveness. All those who had slighted her in the past were killed, imprisoned, tortured or blinded. That included her co-wives and children and relatives and associates, irrespective of rank or status. Meanwhile, this was how Rukn-ud-din's 'rule' looked like, in the words of Siraj:

> The new monarch opened the doors of his treasury and gave himself up to pleasure, squandering public wealth in improper places. So devoted was he to licentiousness and debauchery that the business of the State was neglected ... all his lavishness sprang from his inordinate addiction to sensuality, pleasure, and conviviality. He was so entirely devoted to riot and debauchery, that he often bestowed ... rewards on bands of singers, buffoons, and catamites ... he would ride out drunk upon an elephant through the streets and bazars, throwing tankas of red gold around him...[64]

His end was swift. Razia deftly capitalised on his ineptitude and exploited the wave of fury he had caused. By November, he was jailed and then executed and replaced by a triumphant Razia, whose sagacity and political acumen astonished even the nobles and the ulema. The murmurs of resentment didn't take long to surface. Although she was endowed with all the qualities befitting a king, 'she was not born of the right sex, and so in the estimation of men all these virtues were worthless.' Ignoring this inborn disqualification—womanhood—Razia went ahead and committed two major blunders: she began to dilute the power of the dreaded

---

[64] Minhaju-s Siraj, "Tabaqat-i-Nasiri," 332.

clique of the Turkish nobles whom Aibak and Iltutmish had so carefully nurtured; and she began to dress in public unbefitting a Muslim woman: no veil, no traditional garments and refused the seclusion of the zenana. The united nobility with the support of the ulema eventually threw her in jail, and she was murdered sometime in 1240.

The nobility then installed her half-brother, Muiz-ud-din Bahram who quickly became unpopular and was murdered by his own army in 1242. Another puppet sultan followed. Ala-ud-din Masud, the son of Rukn-ud-din Firoz, who quickly followed his father's footsteps and earned notoriety for depravity and inordinate wine-drinking. He was deposed in 1246 and probably murdered in the same year.

Then the Mongols plundered Lahore. The same year.

All this while, Balban keenly observed these sordid developments from the sidelines with quiet approval, tacit participation and muted joy at the kind of brood that Iltutmish, his deceased master, had sired and the degenerate habits they had acquired during their upbringing in a typical royal Muslim household.

The last puppet

Things had gone too far. Lahore was a wake-up call.

Once again, a semblance of stability-through-remote-control was restored in 1246 when the nobles lodged Nasir-ud-din Mahmud[65] as the sultan. He was Iltutmish's grandson from his eldest son who had prematurely died as governor of Bengal. From the moment he ascended the throne, Nasir-ud-din knew that he was and would remain

---

[65] It is in Nasir-ud-din Mahmud's honour that Minhaju-s Siraj named and dedicated his chronicle, *Tabaqat-i-Nasiri*.

a cipher, not a sultan. The real power was concentrated in the hands of the same dreaded clique of the 'Turkish Forty'. More than anybody else, Balban knew it the best. He was at its head. He was also the father-in-law[66] of Sultan Nasir-ud-din Mahmud.

The new sultan quickly gained a reputation as an unambitious, docile, gentle and, above all, a *pious* Muslim king. Fables and legends to this effect quickly took wings. One such fable[67] is that he copied the Quran by hand in elegantly calligraphed script and therefrom earned his meals. However, Nasir-ud-din Mahmud was also pragmatic: he was fully aware of his own deficiencies in confronting the might of the Forty. Which is also why he wisely appointed Balban as the *naib-i-mamlikat*[68], or viceory, in 1249. The same year, Balban married off his daughter to the sultan, a reminder that the sultan was in his debt. The entire administration was now in Balban's thrall and he appointed his favourites—brothers and cousins and friends—to important administrative positions. Almost all the upper echelons of the sultanate were monopolised by Turkic Muslims, a fact that immediately incensed the non-Turkic Muslim elements. They formed a powerful opposition led by a eunuch named Imad-ud-din Rihan (or Raihan), a former Hindu converted to Islam. Rihan began poisoning Nasir-ud-din's

---

[66] Historian and scholar Peter Jackson describes Balban's machination as follows: 'Balaban, whose daughter the sultan married and who acted as viceroy (na'ib) ... until Mahmud Shah's death, seems to play Earl Godwin to Mahmud Shah's Edward the Confessor.' See Jackson, *The Delhi Sultanate: A Political and Military History*, 48.

[67] See: (1) Briggs, "Nasir-ood-deen Mahmood," in *The History of the Rise of the Mahomedan Power in India till the Year A.D. 1612*, Vol. 1, 233–47. (2) Minhaju-s Siraj, "Tabaqat-i-Nasiri," 365 onwards. (3) "The Slave Kings – The Turks Enter Delhi – 1206–1290 A.D.," in *History of India*, Vol. 3, ed. A.V. Williams Jackson, 82–4.

[68] Literally, regent.

ears about the sorry figure that he, the sultan, had been reduced to by Balban. With adequate doses and time, the provocation worked. Overnight, Rihan was elevated to the position of a *wakildar*, the sultan's direct deputy.[69] That meant that the administration of the royal orders passed into his hands. In 1253, Nasir-ud-din relegated Balban and most of his appointees to faraway provinces, and it was now Rihan's turn to appoint his own favourites. However, Rihan was destined to fail and he did.

In just one year.

Balban would show the sultan himself the true extent of the power of the deadly Forty.

I have seen that God caused the sun of empire to shine in the mansion of the Turks, and turned the heavenly spheres around their dominion, and named them Turk, and gave them sovereignty, and made them kings of the age, and placed the reins of the people of the time in their hands.[70]

Historical records don't reveal to us whether Balban had read these lines written by the 11th-century lexicographer, scholar and inveterate Turkic racist, Mahmud al-Kashgari. However, the fact that Balban shared his exact sentiment about Turkic racial superiority is beyond doubt.

The first stirrings of resentment against Imad-ud-din Rihan's authority came, obviously, from the Turkic nobles in

---

[69] Srivastava gives the designation as prime minister (*The Sultanate of Delhi*, 110); Majumdar translates it as 'Superintendent of the King's Household establishment' (*The History and Culture of the Indian People*, Vol. 5, 190); Jackson translates it as 'Comptroller of the King's household' (*The Delhi Sultanate: A Political and Military History*, 42).

[70] Quoted in Crowley, *1453: The Holy War for Constantinople and the Clash of Islam and the West*, 28.

the sultan's court. The fact that a lowly Indian Muslim[71] like Rihan could even reach such a high office reveals another vital fact and outcome of the Turkic Muslim invasions of India and the subsequent establishment of the Delhi Sultanate. These invasions had created an entirely new class of Muslims in India—converted forcibly or at the point of a sword—whose number was rapidly growing and with it, their political ambitions. They were generally known as the neo-Muslims, a term of contempt. The coveted throne of the sultan or even life as a noble, officer or a high-ranking courtier fired their dreams. Their Turkish masters had themselves shown the way. All it took was to emulate them: in dress, manners, customs, speech. And methods. And tactics. Intrigues, plotting, conspiracy, back-stabbing, murder—whatever it took. Indeed, if the entire Muslim world was a universal brotherhood of Islam where all Muslims were equal, aspiration for the sultanate was a valid form of expressing and attaining the same brotherhood. However, the stranglehold of the foreign Turkic Muslims was absolute, ruthless and brutal. And they made no pretence of their open hostility to Indian Muslims. Even the notion of an Indian Muslim holding any position of authority in the administration was revolting and intolerable. The intensity of their revulsion for Indian Muslims almost equalled their hatred for the infidel Hindus.

Imad-ud-din Rihan would learn his lesson painfully.

First, the language. Chroniclers like Minhaju-s Siraj who lost their lucrative and powerful jobs the day Rihan took over, liberally heap abusive language related to his birth: 'baseborn Indian eunuch', 'Hindi ruler', 'renegade Hindu',

---

[71] The chronicler Zia-ud-din Barani calls Indian Muslims 'dogs', 'low born' who are 'capable of only vices' and says the 'precious stones' of the Islamic scripture were not to be taught to them. Zia-ud-din Barani, *Fatawa-i-Jahandari*, English trans. by Afsar Begum and Mohammad Habib (Allahabad: Kitab Mahal, 1960), 49, 98.

'vile upstart', 'conspirator', 'usurper', 'scoundrel', 'impotent', 'overthrower of ancient laws', 'obnoxious' and 'rascal'. Minjhaju-s Siraj writes a liminal account of the agonising months spent by members of the glorious Turkic nobles now relegated to powerlessness and irrelevance.

> [L]ike fish out of water, and sick men without slumber, from night till morn, and from morn till night, they offered up their prayers to the Creator, supplicating him to let the dawn of Ulugh Khan's prosperity break forth in splendour, and dispel with its brilliant light the gloom occasioned by his rival Rihan. The Almighty graciously gave ear to the prayers.... *The nobles and servants of the State were all Turks of pure origin and Taziks of good stock, but 'Imddu-d din was an eunuch and impotent; he, moreover, belonged to one of the tribes of Hindustan. Notwithstanding all this he exercised authority over the heads of all these chiefs* [emphasis added]. They were disgusted with this state of affairs and could no longer endure it. They suffered so much from the hands of the bullies who were retained by 'Imadu-d din, that for six months they could not leave their houses, nor could they even go to prayers on Fridays. *How was it possible for Turks and Maliks, accustomed to power, rule, and warfare, to remain quiet under such ignominy?* [emphasis added][72]

Without wasting much time, these pure-origin Turks and Tajiks beseeched Balban and formed a tight and determined confederacy. They offered their armies under Balban's leadership, giving him absolute authority to take action as he pleased. The accursed Rihan had to be removed at any cost. In 1254, the substantial force moved towards Delhi. Nasir-ud-din Mahmud began to panic when he realised that the Turkic officers and chieftains posted in

---
[72] Minhaju-s Siraj, "Tabaqat-i-Nasiri,", 371.

the vicinity of Delhi had united under Balban. However, he took Rihan's advice to face Balban head-on and set out from Delhi. Too little too late. When the two armies met at Samana, there was an uneasy face-off. Nasir-ud-din blinked first. Three or four days later, Balban sent out a polite threat to the sultan: the united Turkic malcontents were all ready to obey His Majesty, provided the rascal Imad-ud-din Rihan would be immediately stripped of all his power. His Majesty agreed. Rihan was banished to faraway Bahraich. Balban had regained his former position without shedding a drop of blood and 'shone forth with brilliant radiance'.[73] The dreaded Forty had brought the Delhi sultan himself to his knees.

A year later, Rihan was put to death. The same year, sultan Nasir-ud-din Mahmud died of natural causes—some chroniclers[74] suspect that Balban had poisoned him. The sultan didn't have any male heir. The lineage of Iltutmish was extinguished. Balban usurped the throne unopposed. The de facto ruler of twenty years was formally enthroned as Sultan Ghiyas-ud-din Balban in 1266. It was the beginning of another ephemeral but the last Mamluk Slave dynasty.

'It was the will of God that Balban should excel them all'

As someone who not only hailed from the dreaded Forty, the self-serving and scheming class of Turkish nobility at the Delhi Sultanate, but was also its leader and chief schemer, Balban had an unmatched understanding of how this toxic conspiratorial system worked. So the first thing he did after becoming sultan was systematically demolish it through a series of deft measures.

---

[73] Ibid., 373.
[74] For example, Ibn Batuta and Isami.

Balban's zeal as a committed and fanatical Sunni Muslim sultan surpassed even that of Iltutmish. For decades, he had evolved his own brand of a military despotism that had the full sanction of his religion. All these decades, he silently watched with appalled outrage the manner in which this powerful Turkish nobility had degraded the respect, prestige, status and awe that the sultan's throne must ideally command, forgetting that he was himself at the summit that enabled this degradation. But now, *sultan* Balban was akin to a piously despotic version of Polonius to the limited extent that he waxed eloquently and elaborately on the way an empire must be run. According to the historical scholar A.L. Srivastava,

> [Balban] emphasized on the sacredness of the king's person. He believed in his inherent despotism. His conviction was that unalloyed despotism alone could exact obedience ... from his subjects and ensure the security of the State.[75]

But Balban had to muster more forbidding credentials to ensure this sanctity of His Person. Unlike his deceased master and predecessor Iltutmish, who had successfully obtained the Caliph's blessings, Balban sought legitimacy for his own usurpation from other sources. He belonged in a Higher Realm. The outcome was the invention of a fantastic myth about his origins. As it stood, there was an ample supply of myth-makers and hagiographers, like Minhaju-s Siraj and the ulema and other members of the clergy who would gladly perpetuate the myth. And so it was created: Sultan Ghiyas-ud-din Balban had actually descended from the warrior bloodline of the ancient Turkish[76] mythical hero, Afrasiab of Turan.

---

[75] Srivastava, *The Sultanate of Delhi*, 115–6.
[76] Persian, according to some accounts. See, for example, Lal, *The Legacy of Muslim Rule in India*, 55; see also, Srivastava, *The Sultanate of Delhi*, 116.

His former friends and peers and co-conspirators of the (erstwhile) Forty noted with growing alarm the sudden and shocking changes that he began making at breakneck speed.

Sultan Ghiyas-ud-din Balban was no longer accessible to them. The studied demeanour of cultivated regal gravity and imperial distance had an element of dread instilled in it. To heighten this dread, he imported tall, hefty, seasoned and battle-hardened barbarians from Central Asia who formed an imposing flank around His Person with their enormous swords drawn in readiness, dazzling in the sun, each time he stepped out of his private chambers. Next was the manner in which he transformed his entire court into a sprawling den of puritanical, political Islam. Anything deemed even remotely un-Islamic or non-Sharia was ruthlessly prohibited. Wine drinking was the first casualty. The perennial taps supplying on-demand intoxication to his courtiers, nobles, chiefs and officials dried up overnight because liquor making was outlawed. Music was banned. Entertainment was a punishable offence. It was even dangerous to laugh or smile in His Presence. They were nobles and chiefs assigned to the weighty and pious task of ensuring the preservation, consolidation and, where possible, extension of Islam's dominions in this vast infidel land, and they had to play the part seriously. Court etiquette was strictly enforced on the model set by the grand and ostentatious Persian kings with additional ceremonial ingredients imported from the Seljuks and Khwarezmians. The appropriate dress code befitting the courtier's rank and station had to be compulsorily worn during business hours. Leading by example, Balban did not permit even his private attendants to see him without his *yakta,* the royal jacket. Even the *notion* of relaxation or deviation from these norms didn't arise. The strict conventions of royal salutation had to be adhered to: doing the *sajda* (prostration) and *paibos* (kissing the sultan's feet) were inseparable elements of this decorum. To enhance the ornate splendour, pomp and ostentation of the sultan's court, he introduced the annual Persian festival of Navroz, marking the vernal equinox. Firishta paints a rather vivid portrait of the whole ceremony.

> So imposing were the ceremonies of introduction to the royal presence, that none could approach the throne without a mixture of awe and admiration. Nor was Ghiyas-ud-din Balban less splendid in his processions. His state elephants were covered with purple and gold trappings. His horseguards, consisting of a thousand Tartars, appeared in glittering armour, mounted on the finest steeds of Persia and Arabia, with silver bits, and housings of rich embroidery. Five hundred chosen foot, in rich liveries, with drawn swords, preceded him, proclaiming his approach, and clearing the way. His nobles followed according to their rank, with their various equipages and attendants.[77]

The transformation was complete. Sultan Ghiyas-ud-din Balban had no equal in the Allah-bestowed dominion over which he lorded with an iron fist. Nobles and chiefs below a certain rank were not allowed to even approach him. When Fakr Bawni, an incredibly rich merchant from Delhi, offered him all his wealth just so he could have the great honour of just a few moments of audience with His Highness, Balban refused. Bawni was merely a *malik-ut-tujjar*, the chief of merchants. Meeting such a low man would 'compromise the dignity of the sovereign'[78].

As the calescence of his imperial and unbridled power intensified, so did his unshakeable belief in the god-given

---

[77] Briggs, *History of the Rise of the Mahomedan Power in India till the Year A.D. 1612*, Vol. I, 252.
[78] Chandra, *Medieval India: From Sultanat to the Mughals–Delhi Sultanat (1206–1526)*, 55.

supremacy of the Turkic people as The Chosen Ones. To the maximum extent possible, Balban purged his administration of non-Turkic Muslims and imposed an unspoken ban on hiring Indian Muslims in state service. In one instance, he dealt a stern rebuke to an officer for having employed a native Muslim as a clerk in the district office at Amroha. This pithy analysis provides a representative picture of Balban's incurable racism in favour of the Turkic people:

> Balban ... employed his extraordinary energy and will-power to perpetuate a racial polity which, in, its ultimate form, merged with his absolutism. He symbolized the primacy of the Turk, with his own power exercised primarily in the interest of his race. Expansion of the kingdom was therefore of less immediate importance than perfecting the coercive instrument with which to vindicate this superiority.[79]

Balban's consistent attitude towards and refrain regarding non-Turkic Muslims was couched in just one term: *low birth*.

Decimation of the dreaded Forty

And now, Sultan Ghiyas-ud-din Balban turned his attention to the members of the Forty. Unlike the cautious and measured Iltutmish, he had extraordinary confidence in his own abilities as a ruthless imperialist. Given how he had transformed the throne of the sultan as absolute and irrefragable, he no longer needed to humour the Forty. However, he also knew that they derived their power by working as a predatory pack, which had carved out of the sultanate neat little islands of power, pelf, office, influence

---

[79] Majumdar, *The History and Culture of the Indian People*, Vol. 5, 152.

and loyalists at all levels of officialdom. This was precisely how they had kicked around all the previous puppet 'sultans', including Nasir-ud-din Mahmud. Besides, like Balban himself, all the other thirty-nine were slaves of Iltutmish.

It was time to scrub them clean.

Balban adopted a highly effective and ruthless triad of administrative intrigue to implement this sweeping purge. The first was to completely sideline the Forty by promoting junior Turkic Muslims on an equal footing. This had the immediate psychological impact of reducing the clique's prestige, even relevance, in the eyes of the public. The second was to mercilessly inflict the full might of the sultan's punishing power on them for the slightest lapse, both real and imagined. The first and the second were accomplished through the third and the most effective of all: instituting an elaborate, well-oiled and lethal spy system, which companioned the other powerful institution: the military.

For the Forty, this unfolded in a nightmarish fashion. Malik Baqbaq, the governor of Badaun, was one of the early victims. For long, he had enjoyed prestige as a powerful member of this clique, maintaining a 'guard of 1000 horsemen'. On a fateful day, he had a servant beaten to death for a minor infringement. The complaint reached Balban, who acted instantly. Baqbaq was publicly flogged to death. And because his *baird* (spy) at Badaun had not reported the matter to Balban the moment it had occurred, he too was publicly hanged to death. Haibat Khan, the governor of Awadh, was next. He was guilty of a similar crime: killing a servant while being severely drunk on wine. Balban had him publicly whipped, a grand total of five hundred lashings. Abject humiliation followed. Haibat was made the slave of the widow of the slain servant and was finally released from bondage after he paid twenty thousand silver *tankas*. Overwhelmed with shame and humiliation,

Haibat Khan locked himself up in his home and died alone, wallowing in ignominy and misery. Next came Amin Khan's turn. Balban had deputed him to quell the rebellion of the wily upstart Tughril, his former governor of Bengal, who had declared independence. Amin Khan spectacularly failed in the endeavour and was publicly hanged to death on the gates of the ancient city of Ayodhya. Then it was the turn of Sher Khan, his own cousin. His only crime was that he commanded the respect of the Forty on the merit of his competence, smartness and efficiency. Balban had him[80] poisoned. Even a whiff of competition was dangerous and therefore intolerable. Sher Khan's death removed the last challenge to Balban's despotic supremacy. More dismissals, exiles and deaths followed.

By 1276, the Forty had ceased to exist.

As the former member of the Forty, Balban had understood very early that conspiracies and intrigues against the sultan could never really be stopped. After all, Balban had been the most astute practitioner of this dark art when he had, step by step, become the shadow sultan to Nasir-ud-din Mahmud. Prevention was key. For which incessant, wakeful vigil was paramount. In this, information was the most valuable weapon. Almost immediately after Balban had asserted his might and stature as sultan, he invested an enormous sum of money and time in establishing an extraordinary and ruthless spy system, which would prove enduring and would be emulated by later sultans ruling from Delhi. He was personally in charge of this clandestine organisation and personally interviewed potential candidates for the job. He placed more emphasis on character, habits and loyalty to His Royal Person than on the competence of the potential recruits. Competence could be taught and developed over

---

[80] According to Firishta, Sher Khan was Balban's nephew.

time to promising, even average, recruits. The selected candidates were rewarded with handsome salaries and gifts from time to time. Balban's *bairds* or spies fell in the following broad categories: (1) reporters in all administrative departments, (2) news writers in every province and district and (3) all manner of informers who were tasked chiefly with spying on *amirs*. Irrespective of their position in the hierarchy in Balban's murky world of espionage, all spies were made independent of governors and commanders. Every newswriter had to compulsorily transmit news of both insignificant and important occurrences in his jurisdiction *every day* without fail. If nothing reached Balban on a given day, the spy would face exemplary punishment, like the *baird* who failed to report the wrongdoing of Malik Baqbaq.

A campaign of barbarism

Apart from restoring the despotic supremacy of the sultan's throne, Balban made an important departure from his predecessors at Delhi. He did not focus his attention on expanding the still unstable Muslim empire in India through expensive conquests. Past experience, in the cases of Mahmud of Ghazni and Muhammad of Ghori, had shown that these conquests would prove short-lived. Even Aibak and Iltutmish could not sustain their hold for a long time given the constant insurrections. Unlike that of Iltutmish, Balban's plan for consolidating the Hindu territories still under his control stemmed from a twofold motivation. The first was the realisation that in the vast realm of Hindustan, the majority of kingdoms were still in the hands of the accursed infidels, and as a pious Sunni Muslim, even a slight error of judgement would cause the 'destruction of the Mahomedans'[81] at their hands. This is also the reason he made it a rule to never place any Hindu 'in a situation of trust or power'[82]. The second was rooted in his naked racism of maintaining and sustaining the political supremacy of the Turkic Muslim state in Hindustan. Aggressive, unprovoked wars against infidel kingdoms would not only deplete his resources but large-scale deaths of soldiers would also further reduce the numbers of Turks who were still a minority here.

As a sagacious planner and heartless executor, he first surveyed the scene.

From Balban's perspective, it appeared that no part of the empire that he had usurped was free from revolt. Some portions of the empire stood on the brink of permanently slipping away from Muslim control. On their part, the infidels considered their incessant and unyielding uprisings as a freedom struggle. It was akin to the same effort that was witnessed in Gujarat more than a century ago: the manner in which Gujarat had rebounded with greater splendour and vigour the moment Mahmud of Ghazni had left after thoroughly ravaging it. Achieving freedom meant a glorious return to their ancestral culture, civilisation and values, following which would ensure such stability, prosperity and peace. To his shock and fury, Balban now found that the infidels had expelled most of the Turkic governors and military garrisons and had reoccupied them. It was a repeat of what Iltutmish had faced throughout his career as a sultan. Even the surroundings of Delhi itself were unsafe. An entire region, about 80 miles to the southeast of Delhi, had been recaptured by the Mewatis[83] who led devastating raids of plunder and destruction almost daily and terrorized

---

[81] Briggs, *History of the Rise of the Mahomedan Power in India till the Year A.D. 1612*, Vol. I, 250.
[82] Ibid.
[83] Also known as Meos.

the people of Delhi to the extent that the gates of the city were closed shut after the afternoon Muslim prayers. An unbiased reading of history clearly reveals the truth behind their portrayal as robbers and bandits. The Mewatis were a freedom-loving people who desperately wanted to avenge the appalling indignities they had suffered due to Muslim invasions. At some point in the recent past, they had ruled these regions, and the frequent raids into Delhi were among other methods they used to inflict as much damage as they could on the hated alien sultanate. Some contemporary accounts[84] of twisted historical scholarship have painted the Mewatis as arch-villains whose 'crime' was that they fought against their Muslim oppressors. Another branch of Mewatis, who were known as Koh-payah and hailed from northern Alwar, were originally the descendants of the Yaduvamshi Rajputs. These hardy warriors proved an even greater, fearsome and persistent threat. Indeed, Balban had had a personal taste of their toughness about two decades before he crowned himself the sultan. In 1248, he had led an expedition against Ranthambhor, which was easily repulsed by the Chauhans who had recaptured it and then grown from strength to strength. Ten years later, he met with the same fate and cursed the 'infidels of Ranthambhor, Bundi and Chittor' for repulsing him. This time, he had a first-hand taste of the valour and daring of the Mewatis who had not forgotten the earlier loss of their strongholds at Bayana and Tahangarh. Swearing vengeance, they adopted guerilla tactics. They spread themselves across the countryside and organised a powerful armed resistance, which intensified in direct proportion to the weakening of Iltutmish's short-lived

---

[84] See, for example, Chandra, *Medieval India: From Sultanat to the Mughals–Delhi Sultanat (1206–1526)*, 56. Chandra unapologetically endorses the medieval Muslim chronicler Barani's characterisation of the Mewatis as robbers and brigands.

successors. Over time, these Mewatis merged with the surging tide of the overall Rajput resistance against the Delhi Sultanate. They inflicted fire-bolt raids in Siwalik, Bayana and as far as Hansi, pushing towards Delhi itself. An alarmed Balban launched two full-scale punitive campaigns against them in 1258, both of which bombed badly. He had to content himself by burning and plundering a few Mewati villages and capturing some of their leaders. The ceaseless, spirited labours of Mewati valour helped the Rajputs at Ranthambhor rejuvenate their strength and accumulate more territory.

If this was the overall situation in Rajputana when Balban took over as the sultan, the scene in Ganga–Jamuna Doab, and specifically, Awadh, was perhaps even worse. It resembled a daily eruption of rebellion. Turkic governors had been driven out, and the infidels followed an unrelenting campaign of ravaging Turkic territory and preventing land cultivation and revenue collection by the sultanate's officers. Katehar reported zero revenue collection because the sultan's soldiers and officers had to flee the harassment inflicted by the infidel rebels. In the faraway east, Bengal posed an even bigger headache. Here is a picture of the overall nature of Hindu resistance.

> *Our patriotic leaders in that age cleverly followed the policy of plunder and devastation, so as not to give sufficient time to the Turks to consolidate their hold in the country. There was, however, lack of first-rate leadership which prevented them from uniting together* [emphasis added] *and mustering adequate forces to fight and expel the Turks from the country.*[85]

Indeed, it is precisely this lacuna that greatly enabled and contributed to Balban's success in stamping out these efforts

---

[85] Srivastava, *The Sultanate of Delhi*, 12.

at reclamation. The wanton savagery and barbarism with which he put them down makes for gut-wrenching reading.

Balban took the first step in 1266 by sending a ferocious army to crush the Mewatis near southeast Delhi. Firishta records[86] that over *one lakh* Mewatis were annihilated without mercy. That genocide pretty much marked the end of that branch of the courageous Mewatis. Balban's army then chopped off the entire forest region in a circumference of 100 miles, built four strong forts at Bhojapur, Patiali, Kampil and Jalali and garrisoned them with vicious Afghan troops. Then he dispatched an advance army to the Ganga–Jamuna Doab and in a short time, followed it himself. This region had to be urgently cleansed of the infidel rebels who had effectively blocked the strategic routes and 'interrupted the intercourse between Delhi and Bengal'. Balban marched through Jaunpur and Varanasi massacring thousands of Hindus. The horror he inflicted at Katehar was truly ghastly. Balban selected five hundred savages from a special band in his cavalry who charred entire villages in the area. Next, he ordered a wholesale slaughter of the entire male population. Women and children were rounded up and sold into slavery. The whole region was depopulated. This is the scene of this all-encompassing devastation.

> In every village and jungle heaps of human corpses were left rotting. The remnants of the people, lurking here and there, were thoroughly cowed down. We are told by the historian, Barani, that the Kateharias never after raised their heads.[87]

This fiendish ruthlessness and comprehensive ruination occurs as a common theme throughout Balban's political

---

[86] Briggs, *History of the Rise of the Mahomedan Power in India till the Year A.D. 1612*, Vol. I, 256.
[87] Srivastava, *The Sultanate of Delhi*, 120.

and military career. Some scholars have termed this as his policy of 'blood and iron'[88], which, putting it politely, was absolutely devoid of scruples and even basic compassion. Unrestrained and despotic political power that had divine sanction was its only justification. Perhaps the most savage illustration of Balban's policy of 'blood and iron' is his horrid genocide at Lakhnavati[89].

Ruling from Lakhnavati, Tughril[90] was the wily and ambitious governor of distant Bengal, a constant problem area for all Delhi sultans throughout the history of the Muslim period. After earning Balban's favour initially, he made a series of shrewd moves and accumulated wealth by constant incursions into neighbouring Hindu kingdoms and principalities. He saw his chance in 1280 and declared independence, gambling on Balban's advanced age and ill health and the great distance and tough terrain that separated himself from Delhi. Tughril awarded himself the title of 'Sultan Mughis-ud-din'. Needless to say, Balban was furious and sent a force under Amin Khan, the governor of Awadh. The crafty Tughril bribed the royal troops who defected to his side. Amin Khan not only had to face a humiliating defeat but was executed by Balban for his failure, his corpse hanging on the gates of Ayodhya. Two more punitive expeditions from Balban met with the same fate. The sultan now decided to stake everything to achieve the singular objective of punishing Tughril. He personally led a huge force and quickly marched through Awadh and north Bihar and reached Lakhnavati only to find that Tughril had absconded. The rebel had badly miscalculated the old sultan's appetite for vindictiveness. Eventually, Tughril was

---

[88] See, for example, Chandra, *Medieval India: From Sultanat to the Mughals–Delhi Sultanat (1206–1526)*.
[89] Also spelt Lakhnauti.
[90] Also spelt Toghrul.

caught near Hajinagar[91] by a search party of Balban's troops. His small force, which had never anticipated the attack, was wiped out and Tughril's head chopped off. However, Balban's hunger for vengeance was not sated. He turned to the captured supporters of Tughril in Lakhnavati. The medieval chronicler Barani describes what happened next.

> The Sultan ... inflicted a terrible punishment upon Tughril's followers. On either side of the principal bazaar, in a street more than two miles in length, a row of stakes was set up and the adherents of Tughril were impaled upon them. None of the beholders had ever seen a spectacle so terrible, and many swooned with terror and disgust.[92]

Firishta narrates[93] that Balban did not spare even the women, children and suckling infants. Everyone who was even remotely suspected of taking part in Tughril's sedition was slaughtered. Balban also ordered the execution of 'a hundred holy mendicants, together with their chief, Kalandar'. The remaining prisoners were fettered and herded to Delhi in the tough rainy season. Once they reached Delhi, Balban ordered stakes to be erected in the marketplace for their execution. However, after a *qazi* intervened, Balban left them alive, satisfying himself by humiliating them in various ways: public lashings, buffalo parades and, finally, life imprisonment.

But before leaving Lakhnavati, Balban appointed his younger son Bughra Khan as the governor of Bengal. The appointment was wrapped in a warning: remain faithful to the sultan even in your dreams. Else, not only will the impetuous sword of your rebellion be cut down, you, your wives, your

---

[91] East Bengal.
[92] Srivastava, *The Sultanate of Delhi*, 121.
[93] Briggs, *History of the Rise of the Mahomedan Power in India till the Year A.D. 1612*, Vol. 1, 265.

children and every single supporter will share the same fate. The warning worked. Bengal was dutifully subservient to Delhi till the last. The warning worked for another reason as well. Very early on, Balban had realised that Bughra Khan was irresponsible, lazy and, above all, an incurable coward who was mortally scared to even look Balban in the eye.

Thy son's father

However, his first son was anything but. Indeed, Prince Muhammad was the proverbial apple of Balban's eye, his great hope who would continue the dynasty he had founded. Balban's inner Polonius would burst to the surface whenever he met Muhammad in private. Prince Muhammad had distinguished himself in his father's eyes as a daring soldier, a skilful administrator and a viceregal endowed with a fine literary taste. The famed Persian poet Amir Khusrav began his literary career under Muhammad's patronage. All were qualities that endeared him to the old sultan. Balban tutored, mentored and diligently groomed his heir apparent on the secrets of running and administering an empire with eloquence drenched in fatherly love.

> When you shall ascend the throne, consider yourself as the deputy of Allah. Have a just sense of the importance of your charge. Permit not any meanness of behaviour in yourself to sully the lustre of your station, nor let avaricious and low-minded men share your esteem, or bear any part in your administration. Let your passions be governed by reason, and beware of giving way to anger. Anger is dangerous in all men, but in kings it is the instrument of death.... Let the worship of Allah be inculcated by your example, and never permit vice and religious infidelity to go unpunished.[94]

---

[94] Ibid., 268.

That was Balban's last sermon to his favourite son, delivered on the dawn of Muhammad's expedition to punish the accursed Mongols who had invaded Multan. As age advanced upon him, Balban found that he had become inseparable from, and repeatedly longed for, Prince Muhammad. However, the invasion had to be repelled. He let him go only after showering all his blessings and embracing him tenderly, and he parted from his son 'with tears in his eyes'.

Destiny willed otherwise.

After a pitched battle lasting more than three hours, Prince Muhammad successfully threw the Mongol forces in retreat. However, in a badly miscalculated move, he doggedly pursued the nimble Mongols who, on their part, were merely enticing him, tiring him out. The strategy worked. Muhammad stopped at a riverbank to drink water, kissing the earth as he did so, and raised his hands high up in the air thanking Allah for the victory. Too late. The Mongol chief and his two-thousand-strong force suddenly exploded on the scene. Muhammad fought a desperate and badly outnumbered battle in which he was repeatedly hacked and ultimately died after a few minutes sometime in February 1286. Among others, Amir Khusrav was captured by the Mongols.

To borrow from the characteristic phraseology of medieval Muslim chroniclers, the womb of Prince Muhammad's untimely and bloody death contained the seed of Balban's own demise. It didn't take long for the embryo to grow, waiting to spear itself out of Balban's belly. Which it did over the course of the year, spilling over to the next. It took the form of greater sternness and cruelty during the day when Balban discharged his administrative business and copious, lonely tears that he shed each night in the privacy of his splendid bedchamber. Life had become an irksome burden that he no longer wished to carry, but the solid empire of

Islam that he had so ruthlessly secured in this infidel land was too precious to be allowed to relapse into a 'child's toy', which it had become under Iltutmish's worthless successors. Infinitely more precious was his own bloodline and the god-given supremacy of the Turkic Muslims in Hindustan. But he realised that his end was near and he had to urgently nominate a successor. He also realised that he had no choice. And so, Balban summoned the inept Bughra Khan from Bengal and anointed him the successor. Like his father, even Bughra had no choice in the matter: the lifelong fright that Balban had instilled in him had decided the succession. He nodded. However, Bughra detested every moment he spent in Delhi. After a few days, he surreptitiously returned to his safe haven at Lakhnavati—as expected. Although Balban was furious, he knew there wasn't much he could do now. But the bloodline had to be preserved. Now he sent for his grandson, Kai Khusrav stationed in Lahore, the son of *his* favourite Prince Muhammad. It was only fitting that this boy was chosen to continue the dynasty. Which was why the council of Balban's most trusted nobles, aides and close friends, which we saw at the beginning of this chapter, had assembled around the dying sultan in the early months of 1287. Of these, Fakhruddin, the kotwal, and Khwaja Hasan Basri, the wazir, gave their solemn promise to Balban that they would unfailingly enforce the sultan's last will and testament.

Extinction through debauchery

Almost immediately after Balban's death in mid-1287, Malik Fakhruddin, the kotwal, embarked on a daring venture to unseat the twenty-something Kai Khusrav. He succeeded beyond expectation. But then, few people even in the sultan's close circle had known the full extent of Fakhruddin's influence. In the span of a few months, Fakhruddin successfully manipulated public opinion and created an impression among the aristocracy that Kai Khusrav was underage, unfit, whimsical and violent. Kai Khusrav saw the writing on the wall. Sensing that he could be murdered, he ran away to the safe confines of Lahore, never to return to Delhi. For a brief period, Fakhruddin acted like a miniature version of Rasputin and succeeded in installing his puppet, the seventeen-year-old Kaiquabad on the throne of Delhi. He was styled Sultan Muiz-ud-din Kaiquabad, and he was the son of Bughra Khan who had now declared independence at Lakhnavati, awarding himself the title of Sultan Nasir-ud-din Mahmud Bughra Shah.

But as long as Balban was alive, he had kept a hawk-like watch over Kaiquabad, for both practical and political reasons—plus experience. Balban had witnessed before his own eyes the catastrophic outcome of an upbringing akin to what Iltutmish's sons received. Accordingly, he appointed a confidential group of strict and ultra-orthodox Islamic tutors of various hues who surrounded Kaiquabad and 'watched him so carefully that he never cast his eyes on any fair damsel, and never tasted a cup of wine. Night and day his austere guardians watched over him. Teachers instructed him in the polite arts and in manly exercises, and he was never allowed to do any unseemly act, or to utter any improper speech.'[95] All this discipline evaporated overnight the moment Kaiquabad sat on the throne previously occupied by the formidable Balban. By the time he had turned eighteen, Kaiquabad had thoroughly transformed Balban's court into a vast sanctuary of vice and depravity. Clowns, jesters, jugglers, singers, songwriters and actors were suddenly in great demand and were paid lavishly. The

---

[95] Elliot and Dowson, *The History of India as Told by Its Own Historians*, Vol. 3, 125.

price of wine skyrocketed. Prostitutes appeared[96] in the 'shadow of every wall and elegant women sunned themselves in every balcony'. Quite naturally, his ministers, courtiers, noblemen and officials of all ranks were quick to imitate the new sultan's graces. It took less than six months to shatter everything that Balban had so painstakingly, ruthlessly built. The whole administrative machinery crumbled, and the deadly espionage system imploded. The sultanate itself became an object of ridicule and contempt. Very soon, Kaiquabad found even the Red Fort stifling. It was now time to permanently shift residence to the magnificent palace that he had commissioned at Kilugarhi on the banks of the Jamuna, complete with vast and sumptuous gardens. News of this palatial royal brothel naturally attracted like-minded nobles and courtiers who promptly followed their sultan. Almost overnight, Kilugarhi exploded with fantastic havelis, mini-palaces, pleasure gardens and ponds and became the 'resort of all the votaries and ministrants of pleasure'.

The obvious consequences followed. Political power passed into the hands of the crafty and ambitious Nizam-ud-din, Fakhruddin's son-in-law. Nizam-ud-din, the *wakildar*, the keeper of the palace keys, wasted no time in making the sultan his puppet and began a series of adroit intrigues against the old guard comprising Balban's loyalists. In a parallel move, he pitted cousin against cousin. The poison that he poured into Kaiquabad's ears did its magic. Kai Khusrav was summoned to Delhi from Multan. However, he was beheaded en route at Rohtak. Other obstacles swiftly followed the same course. The minister Khwaja Khatir, Malik Shahik, Malik Tuzaki and other barons, feudatories and loyalists of Balban were summoned to the Red Fort and killed. Next, Nizam-ud-din ordered a

---

[96] For detailed accounts, see: Ibid., Footnote 214; Lal, *History of the Khaljis*, 2.

wholesale genocide of the so-called neo-Muslims (Hindus who had been forcibly converted during Muslim invasions) on a phony charge that they had plotted against the sultan. It was now time to make the most audacious move yet. He began mixing poison in various potions and intoxicants that Kaiquabad was addicted to. This is a major reason attributed to Kaiquabad's early death by some scholars.[97] Unlike other ambitious courtiers, Nizam-ud-din was not merely content at being a shadow sultan. He fashioned himself as the true successor of Balban, 'the wary old wolf'. Alarmed at this naked brazenness, Fakhruddin warned his son-in-law:

> Give up this idea of sovereignty.... The imperial purple befits the person of soldiers. You, who dare not strike a green-grocer with an onion stalk, or fling a clod at a jackal, how can you count yourself a man among men and dream of an imperial crown?[98]

Needless to say, imprudent ambition triumphed over ability, culminating in disaster. When Bughra Khan learnt of this dire situation in Delhi, he quickly called for a meeting with his son. The two met at Ayodhya, a meeting that was poignant, a moving reunion of father and son who had long been separated. Copious tears flowed. The father whispered these parting words into Kaiquabad's ears: 'Get rid of Nizam-ud-din now! Else, he'll get rid of you if you waste a moment longer.' The warning did its work. Sometime after he was back in Kilugarhi, Kaiquabad prepared a transfer order: Nizam-ud-din had to take charge of Multan. But

---

[97] Lal, *History of the Khaljis*, 4.
[98] Ibid., 5.

the young sultan's courtiers had decoded the cipher hidden in the 'transfer order'. A few days later, a fatal poison was mixed in Nizam-ud-din's wine.

However, Nizam-ud-din's death created a void of sorts. Whatever little grip the administration had had when it was under his control completely vanished now. Unemployment soared. The already-ruined economy was now wholly wrecked. People 'flocked to the gates of the palace' in a mood of semi-revolt. Law enforcement was absent, and 'no security was anywhere to be found'. On a larger canvas, the proud Turkic Muslim Empire that Balban had consolidated was disintegrating at breakneck speed. The Mongols who had been keenly watching the degenerate Kaiquabad now had a field day. Under the leadership of Tamur Khan[99], their bloodthirsty armies descended upon and ravaged Punjab and knocked the doors of Lahore. The momentary burst of energy and sanity that Kaiquabad had shown in getting rid of Nizam-ud-din soon dissolved itself in his renewed and insatiable pursuit of depravity. Increasingly, Kaiquabad found that his thoroughly ravaged health refused to cooperate even in this pursuit of unbridled pleasure. However, in yet another rare moment of mental acuity and sobriety, this victim of his own sculpting realised that some semblance of order and administration had to be restored. And so, he took a decision that would not only extinguish Balban's infant dynasty almost overnight but irreversibly alter the history of India for the next four hundred years.

---

[99] Not to be confused with Taimur or Tamerlane.

Sultan Muiz-ud-din Kaiquabad summoned a battle-hardened Sirjandar, a noble and the governor of Samana[100], awarded him the title of Shayasta Khan and assigned to him the portfolio of Ariz-i-Mumalik, the Minister of War.

He was seventy years old, and his name was Jalal-ud-din Firoz Khalji.

---

[100] Now a municipal council in the Patiala district.

Bibliography

Akbar, M.J. *The Shade of Swords: Jihad and the Conflict Between Islam and Christianity*. New Delhi: Roli Books Private Limited, 2013.

Archeological Survey of India. *Qutab Minar & Adjoining Monuments*. Delhi: The Director General Archeological Survey of India, 2002.

Atkinson, Edwin T. *Descriptive and Historical Account of the Aligarh District*. Allahabad: North Western Frontier Provinces Government Press, 1875.

Barani Zia-ud-din, *Fatawa-i-Jahandari*. Translated by Afsar Begum and Mohammad Habib. Allahabad: Kitab Mahal, 1960.

Bearman, P. Th. Bianquis, C.E. Bosworth, E. van Donzel, and W.P. Heinrichs eds. *Encyclopaedia of Islam,* 2nd ed. Leiden: Brirs, 1960–2008. Available online at https://referenceworks.brillonline.com/browse/encyclopaedia-of-islam-2

Briggs, John. *History of the Rise of the Mahomedan Power in India till the Year A.D. 1612*, Vol. 1. Calcutta: Cambray & Co, 1908.

Chandra, Satish. *Medieval India: From Sultanat to the Mughals–Delhi Sultanat (1206–1526)*. New Delhi: Har Anand Publications, 2007.

Coomaraswamy, Ananda K. *The Origin of the Buddha Image*. New Delhi: Munshiram Manoharlal Publishers, 2001.

Crowley, Roger. *1453: The Holy War for Constantinople and the Clash of Islam and the West*. New York: Hyperion, 2006.

Dubey, D.P. 'A Note on the Identification of Asni'. *Bulletin of the Deccan College Research Institute* 68/69 (2008): 231–236.

Durant, Will. *The Story of Civilization, Volume I: Our Oriental Heritage*. New York: Fine Communications, 1997.

Dutt, M.N. *Vishnupuranam*. Calcutta: Elysium Press. 1896.

Elliot, H.M. *The Hindu Kings of Kabul*. London: Packard Humanities Institute, 1869

Elliot, H.M., and John Dowson. *The History of India as Told by Its Own Historians*, Vols 1–3. London: Trubner & Co, 1867–71.

Encyclopaedia Britannica. https://www.britannica.com/.

Encyclopaedia Iranica. http://www.iranicaonline.org/.

Frazier, Ian. 'Annals of History: Invaders Destroying Baghdad'. *The New Yorker*, 25 April 2005.

Fuller, A.R., and A. Khallaque. *The Reign of Alauddin Khilji*. Translated from Zia-ud-din Barani's *Tarikh-i-Firuz Shahi*. Calcutta: Pilgrim Publishers, 1960.

Ganesh, R. *Bharatiya Kshatra Parampare (Kannada)*. Bengaluru: Rashtrotthana Sahitya, 2016.

Goel, Sita Ram. *Heroic Hindu Resistance to Muslim Invaders (636 AD to 1206 AD)*. New Delhi: Voice of India, 1994.

Gundappa, D.V. 'The Classical Age', book review broadcast from All India Radio, Mysore, 26 July 1954. Reprinted in *Triveni Journal*, October 1954.

Hansen, Valerie. *The Silk Road: A New History*. New York: Oxford University Press, 2012.

Hardy, Peter. *Historians of Medieval India*. London: Luzac & Company, 1966.

Howard, Douglas A. *A History of the Ottoman Empire*. New York: Cambridge University Press, 2017.

Jackson, Peter. *The Delhi Sultanate: A Political and Military Hiation*. New York: Cambridge University, 2003.

Jackson, Williams A.V. (ed.). *History of India*, Vol. 5. New York: Columbia University Press, 1906

Jain, Meenakshi. 'A Review of Romila Thapar's *Somanatha, The Many Voices of a History*'. *The Pioneer*, 21 March 2004.

Jha, Ganganath. *Manusmriti with the Manubhasya of Medhatithi*. 5 vols. Calcutta: University of Calcutta, 1926.

Kale, M.R. *Raghuvamsha of Kalidasa*. Bombay: Gopal Narayen & Co, 1922.

Kale, M.R. *Meghadhuta of Kalidasa*. 3rd ed. Bombay: Gopal Narayen & Co, 1934.

Khan, K.D.L. 'Ajmer's Adhai din ka Jhonpra'. *The Tribune*, 2 September 2007.

Khan, Muhammad Muhsin. *Sahih Al Bukhari (Arabic–English)*, Vol. 6. Riyadh: Darussalam Publishers & Distributors, 1997.

Lal, K.S. *History of the Khaljis*. Allahabad: The Indian Press Ltd, 1950.

Lal, K.S. *The Legacy of Muslim Rule in India*. New Delhi: Voice of India, 1992.

Lal, K.S. *Muslim Slave System in Medieval India*. Delhi: Aditya Prakashan, 1994.

Levi, C. Scott. 'Hindus beyond the Hindu Kush: Indians in the Central Asian Slave Trade'. *Journal of the Royal Asiatic Society*, 12(3) (2002): 277–288.

Mahmood, Sheikh Zahir. 'The Life of Abd Allah ibn Zubair'. Available at: https://kalamullah.com/zahir-mahmood.html (accessed 18 February 2020).

Majumdar, R.C. (ed.). *The History and Culture of the Indian People:* Volumes 2–5. Mumbai: Bharatiya Vidya Bhavan, 2015.

McLeod, John. *The History of India*. Connecticut: Greenwood Publishing Group, 2002.

Merutunga, Acharya, and C.H. Tawney. *Prabandha Chintamani (Translation)*. Calcutta: The Asiatic Society, 1901.

Misra, Ram Gopal. *Indian Resistance to Muslim Invaders up to 1206 A.D.* 2nd ed. Meerut: Anu Books, 1992.

Muir, William. *The Life of Mahomet and History of Islam, to the Era of the Hegira*. London: Smith, Elder & Co., 1861.

Munshi, K.M. *Somanatha: The Shrine Eternal*. Bombay: Bharatiya Vidya Bhavan, 1965.

Nazim, Muhammad. *The Life and Times of Sultan Mahmud of Ghazna*. Cambridge: Cambridge University Press, 1931.

Nizami, K.A. et al. *History of Civilizations of Central Asia*, Vol. 4, Part 1. Paris: UNESCO Publications, 1994.

Raverty, H.G. *Tabakat-i-Nasiri: Bibliotheca Indica* (Series 272 and 273). London: Asiatic Society of Bengal, 1873.

Ross, Denison, and Eileen Power. *Ibn Batuta: Travels in Asia and Africa*. London: Routledge & Kegan Paul Ltd, 1953.

Sachau, Edward C. *Alberuni's India*, Vols 1 and 2. London: Kegan Paul, Trench, Trubner & Co, 1910.

Sarkar, Jadunath. *Military History of India*. Calcutta: M.C. Sarkar & Sons Pvt Ltd, 1960.

Sastri, Srikanta, S. *Geopolitics of India and Greater India*. Bangalore: Madhu Publishers, 1943.

Sharma, Dasharatha. *Early Chauhan Dynasties*. New Delhi: Motilal Banarsidass, 1975.

Sheikh, Majid. 'Harking Back: Slaves from Lahore and Punjab', *Dawn*, Karachi, 23 December 2018.

Singh, Y.P. *Islam in India and Pakistan – A Religious History*. New Delhi: Vij Books India Pvt Ltd., 2016.

Smith, Vincent A. *The Oxford History of India*. Oxford: Clarendon Press, 1919.

Srivastava, A.L. *The Sultanate of Delhi*. Agra: Shiva Lala Agarwala & Company, 1966.

Suri, Nayachandra. *Hammira Mahakavya*. Edited by N.J. Kirtane. Bombay: Education Society's Press, 1879.

Tajddin, Mumtaz Ali. *Encyclopaedia of Ismailism*. Karachi: Islamic Book Publisher, 2006.

Talbot, Cynthia. *The Last Hindu Emperor: Prithviraj Chauhan and the Indian Past, 1200–2000*. Cambridge: Cambridge University Press, 2016.

Thapliyal, Uma Prasad. *Warfare in Ancient India: Organizational and Operational Dimensions*. New Delhi: Manohar Publishers, 2010.

Warner, Bill (ed.). *A Simple Koran: Readable and Understandable* (The Islamic Trilogy Series), Vol. 3. Brno: CSPI Publishing, 2016.

Index

Abbasid Caliphate, 39, 44, 48, 61
Abu'l-Muzaffar, 84
Adhai Din Ka Jhonpra mosque, 118
Aditya temple, 30–32
   current state of, 32n48
Affan, Uthman ibn, 14
Afghanistan, 45, 54, 65–66, 81, 86, 128, 131
Age of Resistance, 66
Agra Fort, 82
Aibak, Qutub-ud-din, 3–4, 6, 103, 106–110, 112–113, 116-120, 122, 124
Aisha, 10, 17
al-Baladhuri, 17, 23, 25, 28, 30, 38
Al-Biruni, 31n45, 65, 72, 89
al-Din, Ghiyath, 88, 97, 101, 107
al-Hajjaj, Abu Muhammad, 9, 11–13, 17–20, 27, 30
   consultancy with astrologers, 20
   death of, 32
   military expansion, 11
   mission to Sindh, 18, 21
al-Hidaya, 89
Al-Hind, 12–13, 38, 39, 44
al-Istakhri, 39, 44, 86
al-Kashgari, Mahmud, 143
al-Malik, Abd, 9, 11
Al-Mustansir, 133
Alp-Tigin, 45, 49, 79
   capture of Ghazni, 45
al-Taghlibi, Hisham ibn 'Amr, 34
al-Thaqafi, Muhammad ibn al-Qasim, 11
Al-Walid, 32

al-Zubair, Abd Allah, 9–10
Amin-ul-Millah, 54
Amu Darya, 49n1
Anahilapataka, 69, 120–121
Anandapala, 59, 63
Andkhud, 101
Anivarttaka-nivartayi, 38n60
Arab army, 13, 14, 15, 19
Arab invasion of Sindh, 40
Arab Muslim, 16, 23, 37–38, 40
Arab Muslim armies, 23, 37, 40
Arab principalities, 39
Arabian Sea, 64n35, 75
Arabian settlers, 42
Ariz-i-Mumalik, 167
Aryavarta Consciousness, 49, 52, 116
Asadhara, Jain Acharya, 99
Asir, Ibn, 114, 130
Asuravijayi, 34, 58
Aurangzeb, downfall of, 66
Avanijanashraya, Chalukya king, 38
Aybeg, Qutb al-Din, 103

Babur, 2, 3
   invasion of India, 3
Baghdad, 17, 79, 134. *See also* slave markets
Bahram, Muiz-ud-din, 141, 161, 167
Bakr, Abu, 17
Balban, Ghiyas-ud-din, 104, 106, 108, 133, 146, 147–149, 150
   policy of 'blood and iron', 158
Balkh, 47, 54, 79. *See also* slave markets
Baluchistan, 59

INDEX

Bamiyan, 54, 138
Banares, 114. *See also* Kashi and Varanasi
Banu Thaqif tribe, 20
Baqbaq, Malik, 151, 153
Barani, Zia-ud-din, 5, 144n71
Barbarism
  campaign of, 153–160
  connotations of, 48
Barmer, 37, 92, 131
Basmad river, 30
Basri, Khwaja Hasan, 106, 162
Battle of Chandawar, 113, 115, 122
Battle of Ghazni, 47n77
Battle of Kasahrada, 90n16
Battle of Kikan, 15
Battle of Tarain, 97
Bawni, Fakr, 149
Bayana, principality of, 119
Beas River, 29
Bestiality, 113
Bhagavata Purana, 28
Bhakkar, 129
Bharatavarsha, 1–2, 12, 21, 25, 27, 33, 41, 51, 78, 92, 98, 124
  inception of Muslim rule, 40
  war prisoners, 27
Bharatiya Vidya Bhavan, 4
Bharuch, 13, 37
Bhatiya, 59–60
Bhimadeva II, 91
Bhuvanaikamalla, 92
Billah, al-Qadir, 54
Borjigin, Temujin, 128
Brahmanabad, 26, 28, 35–36
Brahmanabad fort, 28
Buddhist stupa, 55
Bukhara, 12, 48, 79 *See also* slave markets
Bundelkhand, 92, 116, 123, 132. *See also* Kalinjara
Byzantine empire, 10, 12

Caliph Umar II, 36
Calligraphy, 5
Chachnama, 15, 25, 33n49
Chahadadeva, 132
Chahamana empire, 92
Chahamana, Prithviraja, 4, 104, 108–116, 118, 130–131, 138, 141
Chakravartin, 61, 63
Chalukyas, 4, 81, 100, 141
Chandawar, battle of, 133, 135, 144
Chandela, Vidyadhara, 80
Chandragupta Maurya, 49, 66, 100
Chandraraja, 110–111
Chauhan, Prithviraj. *See* Chahamana, Prithviraja
Chenab, 120, 152
Chikudar hill, 82
Cholas, 100
civilisational amnesia, 59
Classical Age, 122
classical Hindu era, 52–57
code of war ethics, 41, 63–64
court etiquette, 175

Da'ud, Abu'l-Fath, 62
Dahir, 18–19, 25–27, 31, 33n49, 36, 56
Dakshinapatha-sadhata, 38n59
Damascus, 32 42, 67
Damyak, 102
Debal, fall of, 25
Debauchery, 108, 140, 162–167
Dehlavi, Amir Khusrow, 100
Delhi Sultanate, 2–3, 6–8, 122, 139, 144, 156
  volatile rule of, 3
Demolition of temples and *murtis*, 81
Deva, Ajaya, 122

INDEX

Devi-Swaroopa. *See* women's chastity
Dewalwara temple, 80
Dhanananda, 85
Dharavarsha Paramara, 120
Dharma, victory of, 50
Dharmavijayi, 33
dhimmi. *See* zimmis
Dor (Dhor), 116
Dowson, John, 35, 41
Durant, Will, 2, 80

Egypt, 12, 64, 134
Ellenborough, Lord, 82
Elliot, H.M., 35
Entertainment, 148

Fakhruddin, Malik, 106, 162, 162–163, 165
Firishta, 72, 75, 95, 108, 113–114, 126, 130, 136, 140, 149, 157, 159
Firoz Khalji, Jalal-ud-din, 167
Firoz, Rukn-ud-din, 139, 140
forcible conversions, 48

Gadaraghatta, 90
Gahadawala Fort, 114
Gandhara Mahajanapada, 55
Gandhara School of Art, 55
Ganga–Jamuna belt, 68
Ganga–Jamuna doab, 132, 156–157
Gangrape, 48
Ganguly, D.C., 70
Gauda, 105n5
Genocide, 11, 48, 64, 113, 115, 123, 157–158, 165
  at Lakhnavati, 158
  of neo-Muslims, 165
Ghaznavid, 45, 49, 53, 78, 80, 85, 86, 91, 106

Ghazni, Mahmud of, 8, 34, 45, 47–48, 52–54, 57, 58, 61, 63, 66, 68, 70, 72, 74, 76, 78, 79, 80
Ghor, House of, 86–89
Ghori, Mu'izz ad-Din Muhammad, 88, 114. *See also* Muhammad Ghori
Ghurid, 45, 86–87, 101, 102, 107, 116
Ghurid dynasty, 102
Goel, Sita Ram, 42
Govindaraja, 94–95, 131
Guerilla tactics, 155
Gundappa, D.V., 8
Gupta empire, 41, 51
  downfall of, 51
Guptas, 3, 85
Gurjara-Pratiharas, 85
Gwalior, principality of, 109

Hajj pilgrimage, 61–62. *See also* Mecca
Hammira Mahakavya, 97n31
Hamza, Rukn-u-ddin, 96
Harappan period, 28
Hariraja, 110–111, 117–119
Harun, Muhammad, 22
Hindu code of war ethics, 52
Hindu genocide, 48. *See also* Genocide
Hindu Shahiya, 65
History writing, ancillary development of, 5
Holy Quran. *See* Quran
Hoysalas, 85
Husain, Ala-ud-din, 4, 87n11, 88
Husam-ud-Ewaz, 133

iconoclasm, 78, 98
idolatry, 121–122, 136
  impurities of, 113

repression of, 113
Iltutmish, Shams-ud-din, 3, 8, 32, 107, 124–126, 128
Imperial Islamic Frustration, 37, 43
Indo-Gangetic plain, 66
Indus river, 47
Indus valley civilisation, 28
Iravati. *See* Ravi river
Irtidad or apostasy (crime in Islam), 63
Islam
    Arab armies of, 13
    Caliphs of, 17
    dominance as a world religion, 4
    existence in India, 80
    expansion of, 5
    fire and sword of, 10–11
    glory of, 74, 78, 118
    light of, 105, 112, 130
    mass conversions to, 41
    might and prestige of, 39
    pillar of (Hajj), 62
    rituals (five prayers), 135
    spiritual head of, 134
    universal brotherhood of, 144
    warriors of, 35
Islamic code, 42
Islamic faith, guardian of, 77
Islamic invasions of India, 7
Islamic political tradition, 33
Islamic State, Right Hand of, 77
Islamic system of statecraft, 83
Islamic war, 57
Ismaili Shia Qarmatians, 31
Ismaili Shia rebellion, 135
Istanbul, 79. *See also* slave markets

Jackson, Peter, 134
Jagannath temple, 31
Jaham, Abu-l Aswad, 23
Jain, Meenakshi, 77, 78
Jaisalmer, 37, 69
Jaisimha, 19, 26–28, 36–37
Jamal-ud-din, Khwaja, 138
Jamiu-l Hikayath, 97n31
Jats and Meds, 35–36
Jauhar, 26
Jayachandra, 112–113, 115
Jayapala, 46–47, 54–56, 57, 58
Jerusalem, 42
Jhelum, 102
Jihad, 61
Jodhpur, 37, 131
Jyotirlinga, 72, 74

Kaaba, black stone at, 62. *See also* Hajj pilgrimage and Mecca
Kabul, 44–47
Kadambavasa, 92
Kaiquabad, Muiz-ud-din, 163, 167
Kalidasa, 33–34, 135
Kalinjara, 46, 67–68, 109, 116, 122, 132
Kalinjara Fort, 122
Kamil-ut-Tawarikh, 130
Kanishka, 55
Kanyakubja, 112
Karmanasa river, 115
Karna Deva, 120–121
Karpuradevi Queen, 92
Kasahrada, battle of, 90n16
Kashi, 29, 112–114. *See also* Banares and Varanasi
Kashmiri Hindus, Islamisation of, 34
Kashyapa rishi, 28
Kathiawar, 69, 74
Kautilya, 40, 50
Khalifa, 133–134
Khalifa-yi Amir al-Mu'minin, 134
Khalji dynasty, 3

INDEX 177

Khalji, Ala-ud-din, 4, 135
Khalji, Ali Mardan, 126
Khalji, Bakhtiyar, 115, 123
Khan, Amin, 152, 158
Khan, Bughra, 50, 159–160, 162, 165
Khan, Genghis, 8, 128–129, 130
Khan, Haibat, 151–152
Khan, Hulagu, 134
Khan, Shayasta, 167
Khan, Sher, 152
Khan, Tamur, 166
Khans, Ilak, 48
Khilafat, 104
Khulasat-ut-Tawarikh, 79
Khurasan, 87, 128
Khusrav, Amir, 100, 160–161
Khusrav, Kai, 106, 162–164
Khwarezmian empire, 8, 128, 137
Khwarezmian Shah, 15, 127–128
Kikan, Battle of, 15
Koh-payah, 155
Kol (modern Aligarh), 111
Krishna Temple, 76
Kshatra, spirit of, 51–52
Kshatriya Dharma, 52, 84
Kurukshetra war, 28
Kushan empire, 55
Kutba, 32, 108

Lahore, 91, 93, 96-97, 102, 103, 105, 107, 109, 123-127, 129, 141, 162-163, 166
Lakhnavati, 38, 158, 159, 162–163
  genocide at, 165
Lalitaditya Muktapida, 34, 38
Lalliya Shahi (Kallar), 44
Layth, Yaqub bin, 44
  liquor, 148
Little Finger, 110–112

Lobhavijayi, 34
Lodi dynasty, 3

Madaini, Al, 25
Magadha empire, 85
Mahakala temple, 135–136
Mahaprabhu, Chaitanya, 116
Mahmud of Ghazni. *See* Ghazni, Mahmud of
Mahmud, Abu-l-Qasim, 47
Mahmud, Ghiyas-ud-din, 108
Mahmud, Nasir-ud-din, 104, 132, 139, 141–142, 143, 145, 146, 151, 152
Majumdar, R.C., 7, 24
Makran, 13, 14, 16, 22, 80
Malik, Abdul, 54
Malik, Khusrav, 91
Malik-ut-tujjar, 149
Malwa, 37, 47, 99, 132
Mamluk dynasty, 3, 124n35, 146
Manat, 78n62
Mangbarni, Jalal-ad-din, 128–129
Mansurah, 39, 40, 75
Marra-al-Abdi, Haras ibn, 14
Masud, Ala-ud-din, 141
Mathura, 29, 67, 76–77
Mauryas, 85
Mazda, Ahura, 55
Mecca, 9–10, 61–62, 73, 78. *See also* Hajj pilgrimage
Medhatithi, 50
Meghaduta, 136
Mhers, 119–120
Middle Ages, 8
  military organisational superstructure, 40
  military–religious despotism, 3, 124
Misra, Ram Gopal, 40
Mlecchas, 24, 38, 46, 48, 56, 93
Mongolia, 12

INDEX

Mookerji, Radha Kumud, 7
Mount Abu, 90, 116, 120
Mudabbir, Fakhr-i, 107n7
Mughis-ud-din, Sultan, 158
Muhammad Ghori, 88–92, 97, 99, 102, 106, 109, 110, 112, 114-116, 119, 120, 123, 126, 137, 153
Muhammad, Ala-ad-din, 108, 128
Muhammad, Ghiyath al-Din, 88, 97, 101–102
Muhammad, Prince, 160–161
Muhammad, Sayf al-Din, 88
Mulastana, 28–29, 30, 32. See also Multan
Multan, 13, 28, 30–32, 39–42, 59, 61, 62–64, 64, 68, 75–76, 89, 94, 96, 101, 126, 129, 161, 164-165
Munja, Paramara, 47
Munshi, K.M., 4, 49, 52, 65–66, 73
Music, 136, 148

Nabhan, 'Ubaidu-lla, 18
Nagabhata, Pratihara king, 37
Nahrwala, 69
Nasir Amir al-Muminin, 134
Navroz, Persian festival, 149
Navsari, 37
Nayakadevi, Queen, 90
Neo-Muslims, 165
Nishapur, 110
Niyabat, 104
Nizami, Hasan, 5, 100, 111, 112, 113, 117, 118, 120, 122, 124, 125, 127
Nizam-ud-din, 165–166
Non-Muslims, treatment of, 41
North-West Frontier Province, 89

Only True Faith, 33, 53, 56, 60, 74, 77, 81, 89, 130

Orthodox Islamic clergy, 60
Ottoman Turks, 8

Pakistan, 1, 14n15, 23, 24n32, 25n37, 26n38, 32n48, 44n70, 47, 65, 129n41
Palas, 43, 85
Pallavas, 85
Paramaradeva Bhoja, 67, 74
Paramaras, 85, 132
Parushni. See Ravi river
Perdition, 117, 119
Peshawar, 55–59, 91, 93, 96
political decisiveness, 83
Prabandha Chintamani, 91n19, 97n31
Pratihara kings, 39, 43
Prithviraj Raso, 97n31
Prithviraja III, 92
Prophet Muhammad, 12–14, 22
Pulikeshi, 38
Purushapura, 55. See also Peshawar
Pusalker, A.D., 7

Qarmatians, 31, 61-62, 64
Qasim, Muhammad bin, 7, 12–13, 19–21, 24–38, 41, 43, 53, 67, 88, 99
brutal storming of Sindh, 43
destructive raids at Debal, Alor and Multan, 41
extraordinary planning, 37
invasion of Sindh, 7
plundered the wealth of Aditya temple, 30
skilful strategy, 37
success of, 35
Qubachah, Nasir-ud-din, 126-127, 129
Quran, 4, 10, 57, 104-105, 110, 142

INDEX

Qutayba ibn Muslim, 11
Qutub Minar, 118, 135
Quwwat-ul-Islam mosque, 118, 123, 137

Raghuvamsha, 34
Rai, Baji, 59–60. *See also* Bhatiya Raja Dharma
Ranthambhor, 131–132, 155–156
Raor, 25, 29
Raor fort, 26
Rashidun Caliphate, 14
Rashtrakuta Empire, 47
Rashtrakutas, 43, 85
Ravi river, 28, 129
  religio-imperialist power centre, 1
  religious bigotry, 12
  religious imperialism, 1, 134
Resistance, Age of, 66
Rihan, Imad-ud-din, 142–144, 146
royal salutation, 148

Sa'id al-Jannabi, Abu, 61
Sabuktigin, Abu Mansur, 45–46, 49, 53, 56, 62, 65, 79, 84
Sacred-heritage preservation group, 48n32
Samarkhand, 12, 79. *See also* slave markets
Sanatana Bharatavarsha, 78
Sanatana civilisation, 80
Sanatana Dharma, 114–115
Sanatana Dharmic, 40
Sanatana sect, 114
Sanatana Vedic civilisation, 28
Sarkar, Jadunath, 7
Sassanid empires, 10
Sastri, S. Srikanta, 7
Saudi Arabia, 1–2
Sayyid, 3
Seistan, 44
Shah, Aram, 125–126
Shah, Nadir, 45
Shamsis–Turkic slaves, 137
Shatavahanas, 85
Shaven-headed Brahmans, 115
Shayban, Jalam bin, 31
Sialkot, 91, 93, 129
Sindh Sagar Doab, 128
Sindh, 1, 7, 11, 13–16, 18, 21–22, 24, 29, 33, 36, 38, 40, 43, 44, 50, 60, 64, 66, 75
  Arab incursions, 50
  Brahman dynasty of, 15
  wealth of, 18
Sindhu river, 59, 63, 76, 102, 107, 129
Singh, Kshetra, 132
Siraj, Minhaju-s, 91, 95, 130, 133, 138, 144
Sircar, D.C., 7
Sirhind fort, 94, 96
Skanda, 92
Slave dynasty of the Delhi Sultanate, 139
slave market, 43, 49, 79. *See also* Amu Darya
Slave of a slave, 125–128
Smith, Vincent A., 5–6
Sodha, 92
Somanatha temple, 67, 71, 72, 76, 82
  vandalism of, 72–73
Somanatha, Ishta-Devata, 72
Spain, 21–22, 39
Srivastava, A.L., 131, 147
Sun Temple, 28, 29, 69, 135
Sunja, 88
Sunni Muslim, 62, 104, 135, 147, 153
Supreme Law, 105

INDEX

Tabaqat-i-Akbari, 79, 97n31
Tabaqat-i-Nasiri, 97n31
Taila II, Chalukya king, 47
Taju-l Ma'asir, 97n31, 125
Takshashila, 55
Talib, Ali ibn Abi, 14
Taliban, 45
Tarain, battle of, 110, 115, 127
Tarikh-i Sind, 35n55
Tarikh-i-Alai, 79
Tarikh-i-Fakhru'd-Din Mubarakshah, 69n46
Tarikh-i-Yamini, 79
Tayasai, Malik, 132
Tipu Sultan, 1, 58, 66
Tsang, Hiuen, 28, 31
Tughlaq dynasty, 3
Tuhfatu-l-Kiram, 20n26
Turki, Sirjandar, 125
Turkic Mamluk, 106
Turkic Muslims, 7, 142, 144, 150–151, 162
Turkic racial superiority, 143
Turkic slave dynasties, 124
Turkish domination, 48
Turkish Forty, 142

Udbhandapur, 44, 46
Ujjain, 37, 135
Ultra-orthodox Islamic tutors, 163
Umayyad Caliphate, 9, 39
Utbi, Abu Nasr Muhammad, 54, 56–58, 63–64, 79–80

Vakatakas, 85

Vallabhadeva, 33–34
Vamana, 92
Varanasi, 112, 114–115, 132, 157. *See also* Banares and Kashi
Vijayanagara, 85
Viruddhavidhi-viddhavamsa, 97n31

War prisoners, 27
Women's chastity, 52
World-burner, 87–88. *See also* Husain and Ala-ud-din

Yaduvamshi Rajputs, 155
Yajvapala, 132
Yamin Khalifat Allah, 133
Yamin-ud-Daulah, 54
Yashovarman, 38
Yildiz, Taj-ud-din, 107–108, 109, 127–128
  imperial pretensions, 127

Zabul, 44, 46, 89
  fate of, 44
  Hindu kingdoms of, 3, 40, 43, 49, 52
Zakariya, Bahauddin, 32
Zamzam Well, 62. *See also* Mecca
Zaynab, 12
Zenana, 141
Zimmis, 99, 105
Ziyad, Tariq bin, 21
Ziya-ud-din, Malik (Kazi Tolak), 95, 96
Zubair, 10–11

About the Author

Sandeep Balakrishna is a former information technology professional with a long and successful career at corporations such as Honeywell and Cisco. He is the author of the bestselling history books *Tipu Sultan: The Tyrant of Mysore* and *The Madurai Sultanate: A Concise History.* He is also the author of the critically acclaimed work *70 Years of Secularism: Essays on the Unofficial Political Religion of India.*

Sandeep has translated the legendary Kannada novelist Dr S.L. Bhyrappa's critically acclaimed work *Aavarana* into English as *Aavarana: The Veil,* which is now in its twelfth reprint.

He is the founder and editor of *The Dharma Dispatch*, an online journal dedicated to Indian civilisation, culture and history.

www.ingramcontent.com/pod-product-compliance
Lightning Source LLC
LaVergne TN
LVHW040144080526
838202LV00042B/3024